Peace in Pregnancy

Peace in Pregnancy

DEVOTIONS FOR THE
EXPECTANT MOTHER

KATHRYN ANNE CASEY

Our Sunday Visitor
Huntington, Indiana

Nihil Obstat
Msgr. Michael Heintz, Ph.D.
Censor Librorum

Imprimatur
✠ Kevin C. Rhoades
Bishop of Fort Wayne-South Bend
November 7, 2021

The *Nihil Obstat* and *Imprimatur* are official declarations that a book is free from doctrinal or moral error. It is not implied that those who have granted the *Nihil Obstat* and *Imprimatur* agree with the contents, opinions, or statements expressed.

Our Sunday Visitor Publishing Division, Our Sunday Visitor, Inc., 200 Noll Plaza, Huntington, IN 46750; 1-800-348-2440; www.osv.com

ISBN: 978-1-68192-488-5 (Inventory No. T2378)
1. RELIGION—Prayerbooks—Christian.
2. RELIGION—Christian Life—Women's issues.
3. RELIGION—Christianity—Catholic.

LCCN: 2022934446

Cover and interior design: Chelsea Alt
Cover art: Adobe Stock

PRINTED IN THE UNITED STATES OF AMERICA

For Stella

Thank you, *women who are mothers*! You have sheltered human beings within yourselves in a unique experience of joy and travail. This experience makes you become God's own smile upon the newborn child, the one who guides your child's first steps, who helps it to grow, and who is the anchor as the child makes its way along the journey of life.

— Pope St. John Paul II, *Letter to Women*, June 29, 1995

Contents

Author's Note

I am a mother. Pieces of my heart live on earth and in heaven. I did not know many moments of peace during my pregnancies, even when the pregnancies were healthy and progressing beautifully, but I sought it and in searching for it, I came to know peace even if I struggled to continue to choose the path toward it.

Isaiah 30:21 reads, "And your ears shall hear a word behind you, saying, 'This is the way, walk in it,' when you turn to the right or when you turn to the left." Even when the path before us is not clear, the path toward peace is the path forward.

This devotional comes to you as the fruit of that search for peace through my personal experiences: a history of miscarriage, two prenatal diagnoses, accepting and lovingly embracing a child who I knew would live with physical differences from his siblings, accepting and lovingly embracing the child I knew might not live at all after birth, and the delight of carrying, delivering, and nurturing five beautiful babies. It comes to you through my lifelong love of the Catholic Church, her teachings and traditions, my education in clinical psychology, and my professional work teaching mental and emotional coping skills to youth. And probably most of all, it comes to you through my experience as a woman in a community of women trying to find our way as mothers and wives in a world that does not offer a clear vision of what that means.

Every mother is trying to find her way. Peace is possible. Even in the most difficult circumstances, I saw the Lord hold out his hand with the promise, "My peace I give to you" (Jn 14:27). In the best moments, in my most treasured memories, I accepted it. And as my journey moves beyond those times, I can even look back with joy.

I pray this book will be a gift to you on this phase of your journey, and I pray that the Lord will guide you and bless you with peace in pregnancy.

Introduction

Finally, brethren, whatever is true, whatever is honorable,
whatever is just, whatever is pure, whatever is lovely,
whatever is gracious, if there is any excellence, if there
is anything worthy of praise, think about these things.

Philippians 4:8

You have been entrusted with the greatest gift imaginable: a person developing inside you, protected from the world, nourished and warmed with your every heartbeat. Whether this is your first baby, your fifth, or your tenth, it is a priceless gift. Life changes with each pregnancy. Your body changes: You carry within you DNA fragments from each child who has touched your womb.[1] Your brain changes; the relationships surrounding you change; even your furniture arrangements change as your body grows to envelop this new life.

It is all so blessed. Shouldn't it be perfect? And yet, this gift of God does not come easily. I know women who question daily, "Am I doing this right?" They fret over the risks of eating goat cheese and whether to vaccinate against the flu. Some will not invite friends into their house, flustered by the messy kitchen because their tiredness precludes housekeeping. Some women worry about pregnancy's possible effects on their other children. As your heart expands to encompass your love for your child, so also your concerns must grow. We must weigh. We must measure. We must consider the best path forward, not only for ourselves, but for this little one.

God calls us to himself, inviting us to offer him our heart's concerns (whatever they may be, large or small) and to step outside ourselves through prayer and meditation on truth, beauty, and goodness. These three things, called the transcendentals, are the ideals toward which each of us strives. They have the power to take us beyond our earthly concerns into God's Presence, because he is truth, beauty, and goodness itself.[2]

Throughout this book you will encounter an invitation to find true peace throughout your child-bearing through reflections, prayers, stories of saints who found sanctity through motherhood, meditations on the Holy Rosary and the Stations of the Cross, and the Night Prayer of the Liturgy of the Hours.

When you open this book and turn its pages, I invite you to lay aside the obstacles to peace you might experience. Hold close the words from Philippians 4:8: "Finally, brethren, whatever is true, whatever is honorable, whatever is just, whatever is pure, whatever is lovely, whatever is gracious, if there is any excellence, if there is anything worthy of praise, think about these things."

No matter what uncertainties, fears, or challenges you face, let each page be your invitation to pause and clear your mind, to remind yourself of that which is true, good, and beautiful, and to draw your heart into the present moment, resting in the Father, who loves you and desires to care for your every need.

I

Reflections on Peace

THE UNIVERSAL PATH TO PEACE

Simply defined, peace is the absence of conflict.

We might talk of peace within oneself, peace with one's neighbor, peace within a family, peace between families, communities, tribes, and nations, and peace in the world.

Peace is simple to define but harder to obtain.

Any experience of change (and we are always changing) creates tension as we work to adapt to the transition. In the face of change, we adjust our expectations and our plans. The adjustment may advance easily or with difficulty depending on one's history, personality, and circumstances.

So it is with pregnancy, whose radical physical and hormonal changes are well documented. We change physically in the space we occupy, muscular ability, agility, energy, and hormones. Emotions, which lie at the internal intersection of our physical being and our spiritual being, are radically affected by these changes. This is the common experience of all women in pregnancy.

The universal experience of adapting to pregnancy is a rich opportunity to grow in the practice of peace.

The universal path to peace is radical acceptance of God's will. Fr. Jean-Pierre de Cassaude refers to this as "abandonment to divine providence" (and he has an excellent book by that title that can help you know more about what that means generally). We choose to see in our experiences the hand of God, guiding us according to his will, for our benefit, just as we see the changes of pregnancy occurring in their own time, to guide the child in its development.

When we accept the natural changes of pregnancy as part of God's plan, adjusting to those changes becomes easier. When our wills align with the will of our all-good and all-loving God, wanting what God allows for our lives opens the possibility of peace within ourselves, when facing great change within ourselves.

The belief that God is all good and all loving is the basis for this trust. This simple yet elegant perception of who God is and of his intentions is often wounded in a world that struggles to believe in a world beyond this one or openly rejects it.

We can then feel something taking place that is greater than a fleshy biological process. By aligning our will with the will of the Almighty, who makes all things and orders them according to his purpose, we have an opportunity to discover a great deal of meaning in the blessings and sufferings that accompany the everyday experiences of pregnancy. Meaning drives us forward, helps us get up in the morning, and shores up our strength to face whatever the day has for us. In *Man's Search for Meaning*, psychiatrist Dr. Viktor Frankl presents and illuminates this idea. Whether we face the anxiety that occurs even in a comfortable family life or in life-threatening circumstances, finding meaning can give us the material we need to keep moving forward with courage.

> *How does this pregnancy fit on the path of your vocation or the plans you have seen God have for you?*
>
> *How does it fit within your own plans?*

Sometimes our answers to these questions are not neat and tidy. Sometimes they do not seem like answers or opinions we *should* have.

That's actually okay. Until we are willing to look at a situation for what it is, with honesty, we cannot find peace. If the answers do not sound pretty, there may be some work to do, but it does not mean that you, your motherhood, or your child are any less beautiful in the eyes of God.

YOUR UNIQUE PATH TO PEACE

In the previous reflection, we considered the path to peace that is common to all.

But you, dear reader, are unique in this universe. Your history, your personality, and your circumstances affect how you will experience this effort to align your will with God's will and accept the change and uncertainty that come with the normal experience of childbearing.

Have you experienced loss? trauma? wounds from your own childhood? Name them.

Be open to observing how they arise in this new stage of this new pregnancy.

Silencing them before listening to them will not make them go away.

Rather, whenever we turn to the Lord to guide us, he wants to gently pull back the layers of our heart that hold the wounds we've carried. He wants to heal us. He will use these opportunities to do so, if we allow him and ask him to walk with us as we explore our history.

You might examine your own history in prayer after reading this reflection, or in a conversation with a trusted friend, or with a trained therapist. However you look into your history, trust the words from Romans 8:28: "We know that in everything God works for good with those who love him, who are called according to his purpose."

Personality shows itself from early on in our development. It is innate, born as part of us, and then develops further through experience. One approach to personality, called the four temperaments, considers how intensely we respond to events and how long that reaction persists. To learn more about them, *The Temperament God Gave You*, by Art and Laraine Bennett, is an excellent resource.

For now, let's focus on these questions:

How do you react to the changes taking place in your body?

Do these changes affect you intensely or lightly, or perhaps not at all?

Does your reaction tap into a longer story of your life that you feel urged to explore? Or does your reaction feel more like its own experience?

Do those around you and their well-being weigh on you as pregnancy demands more of your mental and emotional bandwidth?

Each stage of pregnancy will likely ask you to return to these questions. But when it comes to personality, your usual pattern of reaction and motivation stays somewhat steady. Knowing what makes you tick and how intensely things affect you can go a long way in helping you adjust to internal and external shifts.

Your current circumstances are so unique that this book could cover pages and pages with questions to identify who you are. But you know who you are.

If this is your first pregnancy, what are your ideal pregnancy and circumstances?

How do your present circumstances meet or not meet that ideal? Is your ideal realistic and within reach?

What could be done to help? Is there someone who can help?

If this is not your first pregnancy, what makes this pregnancy unique from your previous pregnancies?

How does that uniqueness help?

How does that make this pregnancy more challenging?

What is your ideal pregnancy? Is your ideal realistic and within reach?

What could be done to help? Is there someone who can help?

These questions help us in our search for peace because where emotion, thought, and will meet in our minds, we have a lot to consider to get them aligned! Our emotions may be in upheaval because of hormonal changes, even though we know intellectually that all is well. Or we know that we are in a bad situation, but we feel surprisingly calm inside. Sometimes we feel anxiety because our ideal is so far from our reality. Sometimes we feel anger, too.

However you answer those questions for yourself, your answers are part of your experience and your circumstances. Our Lord is leading you on this path to help you become the type of mother you were born to be. With the guidance of the Holy Spirit in prayer and some good, frank conversations, you can clear the path for peace, turn to God in prayer, and entrust yourself into his hands.

CLEARING THE PATH FOR PEACE

Clearing the path for peace is an ongoing process, one that we come back to again and again. And so, disposed to accept God's will, working through past trials and tribulations, acknowledging honestly the effect of personality and circumstances on how we view God's will in our lives right now, we come to the next consideration: the personhood of this little one.

During pregnancy, not all tension arises from our internal changes. Much of it comes from the advent of this child in our life.

How is baby's development and health?

What sort of world will baby inhabit once born?

Our body transforms radically to make the best possible place for our child. So often, effort and concern weigh on our minds, as new or experienced mothers awaiting the birth of our child.

What do I need, to be able to give my best to this child?

You are giving so much already.

The concerns and possible anxiety that accompany pregnancy are legitimate. Although this action takes place inside our bodies, from the moment of conception, the moment this child exists, this child lies outside our control. As pregnant women, we exercise control over how we care for our bodies through nutrition, exercise, doctor appointments, and medical intervention if necessary. We do all these things to maximize our little one's potential for success.

Our concern can also be expressed in excess. In a society with massive amounts of information at our fingertips, we find it all too easy to dip into a too-intense, too-demanding, too-consuming focus. For this we must ask ourselves:

What do I have control over?

The rest belongs to God.

And though anxiety can totter into too much, the anxiety we feel as an expectant mother reveals something deep about the world we inhabit. Our love as a mother — eager to pour itself out, willing to sacrifice, suffering through our child's hurt — resembles, as much as any human love can, the love of God for us. For Christ says in John 15:13: "Greater love has no man than this, that a man lay down his life for his friends."

Pregnancy teaches us to watch and wait. We attend to the movements of our baby, ever aware of its growing presence, feeling the shifts and kicks and hiccups. This awareness shapes our mental space, aiding us beyond birth, training us to be acutely aware of our child's whereabouts, exercising that mysterious maternal omnipresence that so mystifies mischievous children.

We grow used to having this knowledge. If — after a doctor's report, a questionable ultrasound, or a medical procedure — we look into the unknown, the pain of that unknown cuts deep.

We might have reasons to worry about our children, those born and unborn. We may have every reason to lose sleep at night, to hold our breath before we hear the rhythmic beating through the doppler or see the movement on the black and white screen. What we do with this concern — where our thoughts take it next — is what moves us closer to peace or closer to suffering.

We suffer when we lack control.

We suffer when we rail against the present circumstance.

Peace does not mean the absence of worry, concern, sadness, or sorrow.

Peace does mean continuing to walk ahead. It does mean that even if we do not understand the reason behind the events in our lives, we trust God is faithful. Saint Paul writes in 2 Timothy 2:13, "If we are faithless, he remains faithful — for he cannot deny himself."

God is faithful, and he will not forget our needs. He made us to love like this. He made us as women, capable of carrying these children in our bodies and in our hearts. We will not do it perfectly. Some days we may not even do it well. But since Our Lord entrusted these children to us, there has to be a way, a way of grace, for us to go forward with courage, hope, and, yes, even peace.

WHEN WORRY EVOLVES TO SOMETHING MORE

Worry, concern, stress all have their place in the movement of a day. A little stress can be good. It motivates us to clean the house, meet the deadline, or stay on top of a child's medication. We assemble the crib for our newborn, remember not to eat Cheetos absentmindedly, or enjoy a new motivation to take a walk or rest when work appears preferable.

Now, imagine stress drawn on a bell curve. The y-axis represents our productivity, going up. The x-axis is how much stress we have, going out. As stress increases, our productivity pushes up. But at a certain point, as stress continues to increase, it becomes overwhelming, and our productivity languishes. We might procrastinate or we might avoid — but for all of us, when we experience too much stress, it hurts.

When the stress response becomes greater than the things causing it, we begin to have a problem. Stress that hinders normal activities by causing us to lose sleep, lose our appetite, or avoid people or circumstances is more rightly called *anxiety*.

What's on your mind, preoccupying your thoughts? Consider taking some time to write your answer out as a list.

What reaction do you have internally as you write that list or look at it completed?

Anxiety originates from different sources: our thoughts, our history, our biology. But we can learn to reframe our thoughts to perceive events in a less stressful way. We can do this on our own or with a friend, a mentor, or a therapist. Some thought patterns develop gradually over time, through experience. Certain events or reminders spin our thoughts to make us believe things are much worse than they really are. In anxiety, our thoughts spin and spin.

Take a moment to listen to what thoughts that pop into your head. Write them down.

Observing our thoughts and writing them down serves two purposes: It allows us to examine their validity and it presses pause on the spin cycle which helps us to regain control when we might feel out of control.

Fluctuations in hormones or an underlying condition can cause anxiety's physical symptoms, even when no actual stressors are causing that response in our lives. Diet, exercises, and in some cases medication are important helpmates in curbing the power of this emotion-reaction.

Do you have any specific physical needs you are not meeting?

What is preventing you from meeting them?

Do you need to ask someone in your life to help you meet them?

When anxiety grips our heart, it can take on a life of its own, as if we are no longer in control but rather are tossed back and forth in these powerful waves — or worse, drowning.

Through all this, Christ is still king. Seeking him, loving him, and resting in him bring us forward, and his Presence anchors us in the storm as we seek the calm of his peace.

But as with a physical illness, sometimes the important next step is to treat the source. Because Our Lord created us as beings with a body, soul, relationships, rationality, and free will, our path to healing and freedom will also involve these dimensions. Treating these dimensions can anchor us, help us navigate rough waters, or even calm the waves themselves, enough for us to take the decisive step forward. Sometimes, we need a therapist.

As you process these ideas and the questions above, consider asking yourself, "Do I need to ask for help?"

The Holy Spirit hovers over the waters, breathing life into our ship. Even if Christ sleeps, he is present; he is with us. In Mark 4:38–39, the disciples cried out and Christ rebuked the storm. He calls us to trust. Ever present, he invites us on to the water. He does not force us to go alone.

THE TIME FOR BIRTH

My beloved speaks and says to me:
"Arise, my love, my fair one,
   and come away;
for behold, the winter is past,
   the rain is over and gone.
The flowers appear on the earth,
   the time of pruning has come,

> and the voice of the turtledove
>> is heard in our land.
> The fig tree puts forth its figs,
>> and the vines are in blossom;
>> they give forth fragrance.
> Arise, my love, my fair one,
>> and come away. (Song 2:10–14)

The hour is coming; indeed it has come.

The waiting time has passed.

Anxiety tempts our minds when something feels insurmountable. The normal response is to mentally anticipate, to plan and prepare for every possibility so that the future is neither unknown nor feels like more than we can face.

The incredible range of experiences in childbirth makes this practically impossible. We cannot hold every possibility in mind. Most likely, it is supposed to be this way.

Experience shapes our reality. Some potential outcomes may never occur to us. There is a blessed joy in seeing what is just before us rather than all the possibilities.

In childbirth, our child's brain signals the hormones in our bodies to move to action. Contractions begin. One after another, they begin to move our baby downward, closer to its place in our arms. For an unmedicated birth, the best way to manage these contractions is not to fight or anticipate, but to take each one as it comes, with its rise and fall, visualizing the good it does by bringing the baby closer, each one a step nearer to meeting your child. We face them and let go enough to allow them to work.

Just as the physical contractions work to bring our babies closer to us, the intellectual, emotional, and spiritual experiences of pregnancy are opportunities to bring us closer to our babies. How we face each uncertainty, each scare, the questions of whether or not we are doing something right, help to train us for this moment. Likewise, how we face each moment of joy, each happy discovery, each new development, add to the internal picture we now hold of this mysterious bond between baby and mother.

You know your child.

Now the time comes to meet your child.

A birth plan helps immensely to communicate your desires to your medical and support teams, but it cannot anticipate everything. Nor can you. It is too much for a human being to hold in mind. Yet God knows the plan he has for you. He knows what you are capable of facing. For all the rest, his power is made perfect in weakness. We cannot be completely in control.

What you can do is fall back on what you have learned in times of prayer, in the search for peace. Rather than holding all the scenarios, hold the prayers you prayed for peace, share them with your support partner, write them, record them, bring them into your mind and heart in the labor process, however you find helpful.

> *Jesus, I trust in you.*
> *Into your hands, I commend my spirit.*
> *Be it done to me according to thy will.*

No matter how much the support or medical people of this labor and delivery are involved in the process, in childbirth, the action comes down to the relationship between the mother and child. Your child speaks to your body, your body speaks to you. Working in harmony, a baby is born.

It is messy, complicated, unpredictable, and possibly the most beautiful and profound thing we can participate in as mothers on earth.

Allow yourself to rest in this knowledge. Rest in the knowledge of the presence of your guardian angel and the guardian angel of your child. Find rest in the knowledge of the women who have gone before you since the first son was born. Rest in the knowledge of Mary and Joseph in the middle of the night looking for a place for the night. Rest in the stories of the saints. Above all, rest in the knowledge of a Creator who loves you and works all things for good for those who love him. Then step forward, allowing him to take your hand, to guide you, and walk with you on this path, wherever it will lead.

God bless you and your child.

II

Portraits of Peace
in Holy Mothers

A community of women naturally gravitates toward listening to and sharing stories of pregnancy. We might compare this pregnancy to our last or to the pregnancies of the women around us. As we connect the dots within the stories that agree, we gradually develop a sense of what is normal among women and what is normal for us. These stories can promote our peace, as they not only pass on information but also build relationships between us, as storytellers and listeners who relate.

When a child is born, we explore the tapestry of the child's face, looking for a physical resemblance from the child to ourselves and to its father, aunt, uncle, grandparents, or siblings. We explore the eyes, the nose, the lips, the ears, and the behavior patterns, piecing together who this child is and who this child will become.

We likewise form a portrait of motherhood by looking at

the communion of mothers around us, whether they are immediately present in our lives, remotely connected through social media, ancestors whose stories were passed down to us, or holy patronesses in the communion of saints. We find inspiration and lessons about what motherhood can become that inform our decisions of what type of mother we will choose to be today. We find hope in the kind of mother we will become.

The communion of saints is not an impersonal catalog of patron saints, but a living community. As you read about these holy women who were also mothers, I invite you to contemplate their motherhood, its place in their journey, and its role in their growth to accept fully the will of God, which is the surest path to sanctity.

THE ENERGETIC HELENA

Stories of Helena's early life piece together tales from historians. Most historians place her birth in Greece, although a medieval tradition points to Britain as her birthplace. She married, gave birth to the future Emperor Constantine I, and as a Roman empress she provided him with his early education.[1]

In her late adulthood, in AD 312, Helena became a Christian. Butler's *Lives of the Fathers, Martyrs and Other Principal Saints* relates, "She was advanced in years before she knew Christ; but her fervour and zeal were such as to make her retrieve the time lost in ignorance."[2]

Upon going into battle, her son Constantine raised the *chi rho* symbol for Christ and won a decisive victory. The following year he proclaimed the Edict of Milan, ushering in a new tolerance of Christianity throughout the Roman Empire.

According to *Butler's Lives*, at eighty years old, Helena traveled to Palestine to oversee the destruction of pagan temples. While there, she founded the Church of the Nativity in Bethlehem and the Church of Eleona on the Mount of Olives.

Through visions and a miracle, Helena located and identified the True Cross of Christ.

From her conversion onward, she continued to be known for her faith, holy zeal, humility, and generosity. After living in the Holy Land and serving the poor in humble clothing, the empress returned to her son. Constantine was with her at her death, according to the historian Eusebius, "caring for her and holding her hands."[3]

Her energy must have been palpable. Travel was not easy, holding positions of power as an empress and the mother of the emperor was not easy, and the search for a relic that had been hidden for centuries would not have been easy. But she did all of it.

It is not surprising that we hear little of her childbearing, but only hear of its effects. Through her motherhood of Constantine, Christians finally found a place in society protected from persecution. Through her motherhood, churches were raised. Through her motherhood, devotion to the relics of the holy cross, the crown of thorns, the nails, and the tunic — tangible signs of Christ's sacrifice — spread throughout the world.

Helena's life began in unremarkable humility, like an average woman of her day. She educated her son and taught him virtue, even if neither of them understood or embraced Christianity until later in life.

She shows us that it is not too late for us.

Her energy made up for lost time. The grace of God guided her steps along the path.

When a woman feels life so intensely, when her whole being aches for action, pregnancy can feel like it slows everything down. Eagerness can begin to erode peace. A woman who carries such intensity might need to be reminded that prayer happens first through silence and stillness, and through action only afterward.

All of these are seeds that will be planted, laying the roots for something magnificent.

In Helena we meet a fellow mother, a woman driven to move forward. For all the heights she reached as an empress, after changing the world, she returned to the smallness of the sphere she had inhabited as a young woman and as a mother. Likewise, wherever we were before now, with the expectation of pregnancy comes an invitation for us to pause, to contemplate, to return to the source of life.

St. Teresa of Calcutta said, "And if we really believe, we will begin to love. And if we love, naturally, we will try to do something. First in our own home, our next door neighbor, in the country we live, in the whole world."[4] Saint Helena shows just how powerful this act can be.

Feast Day: August 18
Patron saint of new discoveries
Saint Helena, wife, mother, empress: You raised an emperor, founded churches, unearthed the True Cross, and then laid all your earthly splendor aside to love the littlest around you. Help me to remember to pause, to accept the physical limitations that may come with this pregnancy, to embrace the opportunity to love, and to keep in mind the providence of God that guides all things. Help me to find peace in the silence and littleness of this child's life. Please offer my intentions at the throne of God. Please pray for my child and for me.

Amen.

THE EMOTIONAL MONICA

Saint Monica was born to a Christian household in AD 311 in Thagaste, a Roman-Berber city in present-day Algeria. She married

Patricius, a Roman pagan, and bore three children: Augustine, Navigius, and Perpetua. Patricius and his mother, who lived with them, converted to Christianity before their deaths. Navigius and Perpetua entered religious life, but Augustine became, as Bishop Antigonus described him, the son of Monica's tears.

Augustine's *Confessions* tell us much about his mother, Saint Monica. In *Saint Monica: The Power of a Mother's Love*, biographer Giovanni Falbo gathers additional sources to tell us more about this mother known for her tears. He describes her as resourceful and prudent: attending to her husband's mood, resisting provocation that might have led to violence, and ultimately inspiring her husband toward truth and goodness by her gentle example, intelligence, and understanding of his nature.[5]

Falbo shares Augustine's own recollections of their days living in community following his conversion, while still a layman, when Monica lived with the community as housekeeper. Her intelligence and quick wit kept pace with these learned men.

Yet the period between this time with her husband and the time following Augustine's conversion exemplifies the power not just of love, but of the way love moves a woman to feel. Monica grieved, wept, and prayed for the conversion of Augustine from a life away from the Church engaged in sexual immorality. Fablo writes that Monica "saw the situation clearly and bathed the ground with tears in every place she went to pray."[6] The Lord did not despise her many tears and would ultimately grant her prayers. Monica appealed to Bishop Antigonus to help her son. Fed up with her persistence, he exclaimed prophetically, "Go away now; but hold onto this: it is inconceivable that he should perish, a son of tears like yours."[7]

She felt her son's choices deeply. Emotions move involuntarily within us. Their movement occurs through biology and intellect, though we are not always aware of the patterns of thought that may drive them. Emotions have the power to move us to act. In different times and places, philosophers and leaders have characterized our passions as weaknesses or obstacles to a chosen goal. To conquer one's feelings was laudable, in their view; to be overcome by emotion was "hysterical." This perspective has long disadvantaged women, with our ever-changing hormones.

Part of spiritual and psychological freedom is the freedom to choose what to do in response to our emotions. Anger or sadness as a result of external affairs can spring us to action and keep us moving in the face of opposition. Fear reminds us to exercise caution. Emotions can be felt to excess or deficiently. On their own they are neither masculine nor feminine, but men and women experience them in distinct ways by virtue of biological differences.

Monica's sadness, expressed through tears, allowed her to turn her thoughts unceasingly to prayer for the salvation of her son. Her sorrow led her to summon all her mental and emotional resources, to adopt a firm attitude of reassurance and tenderness, and to beg for help from powerful bishops. It gave her the inexhaustible energy of a mother in love.

Peace is defined as the absence of conflict, but Christ said to his disciples during the Last Supper in John 14:27, "Peace I leave with you; my peace I give to you; not as the world gives do I give to you." Many still believe that tranquility comes in the absence of emotion because emotions can so often be felt as a storm, perhaps even a storm through which Jesus seems to sleep. But the presence of the storm need not disturb us.

We cannot will emotion to disappear, particularly throughout pregnancy, when it comes to us through hormonal fluctuations and through real concerns for our little one and its future. We lose peace when we lose sight of Christ walking toward us and instead fear we will drown — when all emotions and especially our fears seem bigger than we can handle. If we can rest in the knowledge that Christ is present even if asleep, that this storm will pass, and that the waves of life will calm one day, then we can find peace even in the midst of great emotion. We can allow those emotions, as Monica did, to move us: to plan, to prepare, to seek help and second opinions, and above all to pray.

After many years of tears and prayers, Monica's prayers were answered, and her son became one of the greatest saints of all time.

Feast Day: August 27
Patron saint of wives, mothers, conversions, alcoholics, and abuse victims
Saint Monica, mother of a son who fell far away from Christ before returning and embracing the Catholic Faith, help me to see the value in the waves of emotion so common during pregnancy.

Help me to keep my eyes on Christ, trusting that he is present and has a plan. Help me to see that he is the rock on which I can lean when the storm may overwhelm me. Guide me as I learn how to be a mother. Help me remember that my vocation to motherhood is to be the mother not only of my child's body but of my child's soul, and to pray for my child's salvation, that it will one day experience the beatific vision and see the face of God. Please offer my intentions at the throne of God. Please pray for my child and for me.

Amen.

THE SUFFERING CONCHITA

In her life, Bl. Maria Concepción Cabrera de Armida, nicknamed Conchita (1862–1937), lived as a spirited child, a faithful Catholic, a young wife, a young mother, a grieving mother, a mystic, a prolific writer, and a widow. Blessed Conchita survived a child's death, raised her other children after her husband's death, and endured the Mexican Revolution (1910–1921). As a laywoman, she founded the Family of the Cross, a connected group of lay and religious orders that includes the Apostolate of the Cross, the Congregation of the Sisters of the Cross of the Sacred Heart of Jesus, the Convent of Love with the Heart of Jesus, the Fraternity of Christ the Priest, and the Congregation of the Missionaries of the Holy Spirit.

According to biographer Marie-Michel Philipon, OP, in *Con-*

chita: A Mother's Spiritual Diary, Conchita experienced no conflict between her total dedication to God, her marriage to Francisco Armida, and the births of her nine children. Neither her husband nor her children were aware of the profound intimacy she shared with God in prayer. Like St. Catherine of Siena, Conchita experienced an interior sanctuary. She wrote that Christ said to her, "There your soul will put on wings and the might to go and lose yourself in this immensity of God."[8]

In her devotion, Conchita consecrated her children to the Virgin Mary, writing, "She will be their shield, their light, their guide, their dearly beloved protectress. A loving devotion toward her will save them from all the dangers of this wretched world, so full of perils. Oh Mother, help us, clothe us with the mantle of Your purity, never abandon us until our eternal happiness has been assured. … Oh Virgin, watch over, safeguard them! They are Yours before they are mine."[9]

Conchita did not ignore or set aside the sufferings of motherhood and her love for her children, even in the face of tragedy, as being foreign to the beauty of motherhood. Rather, Conchita embraced suffering as the school of love. She wrote, "I believe the union of suffering is stronger, more indestructible than that of love, the one producing the other. Union on the Cross makes spring from the soul the most sublime and selfless love. It is the purest love, without admixture of egoism of self-love. The love of suffering is the love of Jesus, solid and authentic."[10]

The concept of the Little Way comes to us from St. Thérèse of Lisieux, a contemporary of Conchita. It is a way through life that sees even the simplest actions as opportunities that can be offered to God as acts of love. By committing all our actions to God, regardless of their external worth, we can give God everything as a child does. A child does not worry if the flower is a little wilted, or the drawing a little crooked, or the unexpected sweeping a little dusty; the act is an act of love. Saint Thérèse lived this childlike *Little Way* of love in the cloistered life of her Carmelite convent.

Blessed Conchita lived this Little Way in the home. She lived it in the distractions. She lived it in the physical upheaval of pregnancy, childbirth, and mothering through early childhood. She lived it through difficult in-law relationships; she lived it in a deep love for her husband; she lived it while finding time to pray and write. Blessed Conchita lived the Little Way as a mother.

And we can, too. Each blessed moment and each challenging moment of a pregnancy are steps along the Little Way of love for our child and for God. We can offer these moments as silent prayers, orienting our hearts toward God. We can offer them through our aspirations, short prayers such as "All for Jesus, all through Mary!" or "Lord Jesus Christ, Son of the Living God, have mercy on me!" We can offer our moments through songs and hymns we sing while we go about our day. All of these methods and more can be woven into our day, consecrating each day to God, as Blessed Conchita did.

All of those little actions, even if peppered with moments when we are not at our best, culminate in a life of love. With special papal permission, Conchita died wearing the habit of the order she founded, a sign of her total consecration to God.

Feast Day: March 3

Bl. Maria Concepción Cabrera de Armida, wife, mother, and mystic, help me to see the moments of my life as offerings of love, that I might transform these everyday actions into a consecration of my life and the life of my child to God, who is love. Even though I will fall short, help me to keep before me the knowledge that love "bears all things, believes all things, hopes all things, endures all things. Love never ends" (1 Cor 13:7–8). Please offer my intentions at the throne of God. Please pray for my child and for me.

Amen.

THE VULNERABLE GIANNA

St. Gianna Beretta Molla (1922–1961) grew up with the Catholic Faith central in her life through daily Mass and volunteer work with the organization Catholic Action. She opened a medical clinic in Milan and specialized in pediatrics three years later. Following a pilgrimage to Lourdes to discern missionary work, she met Pietro Molla, fell in love, and married him the following year, in 1955.

Children followed. In *Love Letters to My Husband*, a compilation of letters Gianna wrote to Pietro, we encounter her deep attachment to her husband and her honesty about the daily tasks of motherhood.[11] Her letters express their unity as she describes the way he inspired her to meet the present moment with acceptance and joy. She writes, "Dear Pietro, I could never have imagined how much I would suffer being a mother! I always want to see our children beautiful and healthy, without having to suffer, but instead, there is a little thorn in our happiness every day. ... It's a good thing you're more optimistic than I am, so you can encourage me — otherwise, my morale would be almost below zero."[12]

In her letters, we read about the tiredness of pregnancy, how she missed Pietro while he traveled for work, how her moods changed, and how low she felt at times. She could recognize the origin of some of these emotions and wrote with a balanced perspective, neither fixating on them nor dismissing them.

In her last pregnancy, doctors identified a tumor growing on her uterine wall. She elected for surgery without a complete hysterectomy, thus saving the life of her child. After the birth of a healthy baby girl, Gianna developed a post-operative infection and died on April 28, 1962.

As a devoted wife and mother, a fashionable woman, an athletic woman, a professional woman, a face of the pro-life movement, and an example of a woman balancing working outside the home and caring for her children, Gianna is a modern saint we can relate to — not because of how she died, but because of how she lived. In her life and in her letters, we see her reach out and lean on her husband as her support. Her expression of emotion is honest and descriptive, in a way that we can only imagine regarding earlier saints, whose historical records offer less emotionally candid accounts. We can find it comforting to read a saint who wrote, as she did, "I had a good cry ... then I offered this sacrifice to the Lord for you so that he might protect you during all your trips, and for the baby we are expecting, so it will be born beautiful and healthy."[13]

In her letters, we can identify her formula for peace: Express the feeling, offer it to God, and choose to accept the present moment. Her formula follows what great spiritual masters have written, yet she illustrates these steps for us as an expectant mother.

In Genesis God says, "It is not good that the man should be alone; I will make him a helper fit for him" (2:18). This is not a one-sided help, in which the only the woman helps the man. In Ephesians 5:21, Saint Paul writes "Be subject to one another out of reverence for Christ." This is the support called for in pregnancy. Pregnancy makes us vulnerable.

Many of us are capable of handling the stressors of pregnancy on our own. We are not helpless. Our society puts great stock in the ability to be self-sufficient and not feel like a burden to others. Even as faithful Christians, these ideas can exist in our hearts when we grow up hearing these messages.

But our value as women is not diminished by the weakness

that comes alongside the unborn life of our child. Rather, as Saint Paul writes in 2 Corinthians 12:9, Jesus says, "My grace is sufficient for you, for my power is made perfect in weakness."

The interdependence of pregnancy echoes the relationship and unity of the Blessed Trinity. We grow more like God as we turn toward another person when we are in need and when that person answers our need, because both actions are forms of self-giving love. It is okay to ask for help.

In your pregnancy you offer your body as a sacrifice, made out of love. When you ask for the help you need — whether practical management of the day, heavy lifting, medical advocacy and intervention, emotional support through an open and accepting conversation, therapeutic aid, or assistance from God for your fears — you give others the opportunity to practice virtue and show love. Sirach 6:14 says, "A faithful friend is a sturdy shelter: / he that has found one has found a treasure."

God will give us these places of rest in our search for peace.

Feast Day: April 28
Patron saint of mothers, physicians, and preborn children
Saint Gianna, you were a devoted wife, mother, and doctor. Through the love you expressed to your husband, you show us how the vulnerability of emotion can unite people together. Help me to turn toward those God makes present in my life to support and comfort me. Guide me as I search for the words to share my

experience. Please pray for those moments of vulnerability and self-gift, that they may be fruitful. Please offer my intentions at the throne of God. Please pray for my child and for me.

Amen.

THE PREOCCUPIED ZÉLIE

Marie-Azélie (Zélie) Guérin married Louis Martin on July 12, 1858. She bore him nine children. In the span of three years, four died in early infancy and childhood. All five who remained went on to enter religious life. Pope Pius XI reportedly described Thérèse, her youngest, as one of the greatest saints in modern times: St. Thérèse of Lisieux, also known as St. Thérèse of the Child Jesus. And the cause for canonization is also open for their daughter Léonie.

Zélie managed a lace-making company, and Louis worked as a skilled watchmaker until he sold his business to support her work. Zélie died of breast cancer in August 1877, when her little Thérèse was four years old. On October 18, 2015, Zélie and Louis became the first spouses to be canonized as a couple.

Zélie had it all, in a sense. She owned a successful business producing a craft that required great skill, and her work was in high enough demand for it to provide their sole income. She loved her husband and was loved by him. She possessed a strong faith throughout her life. Her beautiful daughters revered her.

Having it all comes with a price. In *Call to a Deeper Love: The Family Correspondence of the Parents of Saint Thérèse of the Child Jesus (1864–1885)*, we see that Zélie's letters convey the mental burden she felt carrying the blessings of her life. She worried about her newborn, who was living away from home with a wet nurse. She worried about her unborn babies' lives; she worried about her living children's health. She struggled with servants, employees, and family concerns. Devoted to her family, she held their trials close to her heart and prayed for them. To ease her load, her husband encouraged her to send her older daughters to boarding school. She missed them when they were gone, but the excitement of their visits home tired her. The weight of her concerns magnified when her fears seemed justified by a history of infant loss.

A new child undoubtedly brings more factors to take into account. We may find ourselves taxed by the new things to consider when organizing days, weeks, and years. Commitments that we once held in balance now must be renegotiated. There can be a lot to take care of — some things urgent, some not — but with additional lives involved, more tasks seem more important than ever before.

Those to-do lists, those task sheets, the planners, the organizers, and the calendars can all begin to take center stage in our lives. We might research the best possible system for house cleaning, ask friends if they have a rule of life to manage their day, or wonder how to keep appointments when our body has suddenly become a bit unpredictable.

But as Zélie wrote to an expectant mother, "Now the little worries will come, but in the midst of all that, there will also be many joys."[14]

There will also be many joys.

If we, like Zélie, find ourselves preoccupied, then we also find our solution in Zélie's perspective. The weight of what we carry signifies our commitment. Some things may have to change. Others are part of God's plan for our vocation. Zélie knew that if God did not answer her prayers in the way she hoped, her best choice was to accept it.

Many years later, Zélie's daughter, Saint Thérèse, wrote in her autobiography,

> I knew that to become a Saint, one had to suffer much, always aim at perfection and forget oneself. I saw that one could be a Saint in varying degrees, for we are free to respond to Our Lord's invitation by doing much or little in our love for Him; to choose, that is, among the sacrifices He asks. Then, just as before, I cried: "I choose everything; my God, I do not want to be a Saint by halves. I am not afraid to suffer for Your sake; I only fear doing my own will, so I give it to You and choose everything You will."[15]

For the woman who has it all, the path to peace consists in giving all to God.

Feast Day: July 12
Patron saint of matrimony and the domestic church (with her husband, Louis)

Saint Zélie, wife and mother, patron saint of married couples, widowers, parents, and those facing illness and death, you carried on your shoulders the weight of motherhood, marriage, a home, and your work. Please help me to find my way in navigating these new paths, balancing new tasks, loving my family, and embracing the joyful moments when they present themselves. Help me to hold fast to Christ. Even should I find myself longing to simply sit at his feet in contemplation, please help me remember the priceless value of the work I am doing as a mother. Please offer my intentions at the throne of God. Please pray for my child and for me.

Amen.

THE SMILING CHIARA

Servant of God Chiara Corbella Petrillo did not live a famous life. She was like the violets of the garden, as in a reflection written by St. Thérèse of Lisieux: If every flower were a rose or a lily, so much of spring would lose its beauty.[16]

Chiara lived from January 9, 1984, to June 13, 2012. She and her husband, Enrico, welcomed joyfully the news of Chiara's pregnancy. Following the anatomy scan, the doctor diagnosed their daughter, Maria Grazia Letizia, with anencephaly. She grew in the womb but did not have a brain, and the couple was told their child would die during or soon after birth. Against medical advice, Chiara carried her daughter as long as possible.

Her peace faltered after the diagnosis. In her biography, *Chiara Corbella Petrillo: A Witness of Joy*, we read, "She cried out to God. In that difficult moment, Chiara's eyes fell on an image of the Virgin Mary, and everything changed. Peace descended on her heart. She wrote: 'From being condemned to a destiny without hope, I became filled with joy in seeing how the Lord saw this suffering.'"[17]

At her birth, Maria Grazia lived for forty-five minutes.

Their next child, Davide Giovanni, was likewise diagnosed prenatally with life-limiting congenital conditions. Again, Chiara refused to abort her child despite medical advice. Davide Giovanni, like his sister, lived for less than an hour.

During her third pregnancy, this time with a healthy baby they named Francisco, Chiara discovered a growth on her tongue, later diagnosed as a malignant tumor. She delayed her own surgery until late in her pregnancy to give Francisco the greatest chance of a healthy birth.

Chiara accepted her body in its illness and in its incapacity to nurse her son when he was born. She suffered but did not re-sent her body for this reality. Within a year, she learned that the cancer had spread.

Her biography describes, "She always responded that if she could do it, anyone could. Strength comes in making space, in trusting yourself, in truly believing that God is good and that He has only astonishing things in mind for you."[18]

Her yes to the moment was a yes one step at a time.

At the end of her life, her husband wrote to her:

> You know, Cri, I quit wishing to understand, otherwise I could go crazy. And I am better. Now I am at peace; now I take whatever comes. He knows what He is doing, and up to now He has never disappointed. Later, I shall understand. If it happened a month ago, I would not have held up. Now I can do it, if I look at today. Then for each day there is grace. Day by day, I have only to make space.[19]

Chiara died at the age of twenty-eight.

They had lived through this crisis by making space for the present moment. Her biographer wrote, "If they thought about the past, the melancholy would destroy them; if they thought about the future, fear could assail them, because they did not know what would happen."[20]

For all the questions we have that demand answers, we find

at times that persistently analyzing the past or planning for the future overshadows the present. In the moment now is peace. We do not accept God's will based on promising future projections. We accept it because we choose to love him and try to trust him, even when we do not know the reasons for past events or his plans for the future. We trust the words he said to Jeremiah (29:11–14): "For I know the plans I have for you, says the LORD, plans for welfare and not for evil, to give you a future and a hope. Then you will call upon me and come and pray to me, and I will hear you. You will seek me and find me; when you seek me with all your heart, I will be found by you, says the LORD."

If you are facing a diagnosis, whether your baby's or your own, you are not alone. Others have walked this road as well. Chiara's photographs are noteworthy for her remarkable smile in the face of grief, in the face of uncertainty, in the face of losing her life. How could she find joy in the midst of suffering? Her formula offers the key: "The past to mercy, the present to grace, the future to Providence."[21]

Servant of God Chiara Corbella Petrillo, your life is an example of peace, trust, and courage even as the storms of life tossed you about. Help me to understand that the path to peace does not mean difficult times will not arise, or that I cannot grieve or cannot be angry, but that there is a way forward. Please show my heart the way to offer my past to the divine mercy of God, to beg his grace for the present moment, and entrust my future and the future of my child to his loving providence. Please offer my intentions at the throne of God. Please pray for my child and for me.

Amen.

III

Prayers of Peace

ASPIRATIONS

The following are short prayers that you can memorize and say spontaneously to direct your heart and mind to God as you go about your day. Their brevity allows you to pray alongside your tasks.

Jesus, I trust in you!

All for Jesus, all through Mary!

Lord Jesus Christ, Son of the living God, have mercy on me, a sinner.

Jesus, meek and humble of heart, make my heart like unto thine.

Not my will but yours be done.

Come, Holy Spirit!

O Israel, hope in the LORD! / For with the LORD there is mercy. (Psalm 130:7)

"In the Name of our Lord Jesus Christ crucified, I arise. May He bless, govern, and preserve me and bring me to everlasting life. Amen."[1]

"Glory be to the Father Who has created me, glory be to the Son Who has redeemed me, glory be to the Holy Ghost Who has sanctified me."[2]

MARIAN DEVOTIONS

Prayers said directly to the Virgin Mary are powerful aids during pregnancy, as she herself experienced the waiting and expectation of childbearing. You can say these on their own or add them to another prayer occasion, such as a personal prayer time, holy hour, or mealtime prayer. The Angelus is traditionally recited at 6:00 a.m., noon, and 6:00 p.m. Sometimes setting an alarm to say a particular prayer can be an excellent way to help build a new habit of prayer.

The Memorare

Remember, O most gracious Virgin Mary, that never was it

known that anyone who fled to thy protection, implored thy help, or sought thine intercession was left unaided.

Inspired by this confidence, I fly unto thee, O Virgin of virgins, my mother; to thee do I come, before thee I stand, sinful and sorrowful. O Mother of the Word Incarnate, despise not my petitions, but in thy mercy hear and answer me.

Amen.

The Angelus

The angel of the Lord declared to Mary:

And she conceived of the Holy Spirit.

Hail Mary, full of grace, the Lord is with thee; blessed art thou among women and blessed is the fruit of thy womb, Jesus. Holy Mary, Mother of God, pray for us sinners, now and at the hour of our death. Amen.

Behold the handmaid of the Lord: Be it done unto me according to thy word.

Hail Mary ...

And the Word was made flesh: and dwelt among us.

Hail Mary ...

Pray for us, O Holy Mother of God, that we may be made worthy of the promises of Christ.

Let us pray.

Pour forth, we beseech thee, O Lord, thy grace into our hearts; that we, to whom the Incarnation of Christ, thy Son, was made known by the message of an angel, may by his passion and cross be brought to the glory of his resurrection, through the same Christ Our Lord. Amen.

SUPPLICATION

It is good to ask the Lord for what you need. You might make a list of the intentions for which you are praying or the desires you have for your life and your little one. By writing them down, you create an opportunity for yourself to see them as a whole and to offer that whole to God. After such a time or on their own, the following prayers are a beautiful way to lay your cares before the Lord, trusting in his love for you.

Excerpt from the Breastplate of Saint Patrick

Christ with me,
Christ before me,
Christ behind me,
Christ in me,
Christ beneath me,
Christ above me,
Christ on my right,
Christ on my left,

Christ when I lie down,
Christ when I sit down,
Christ when I arise,
Christ in the heart of every man who thinks of me,
Christ in the mouth of everyone who speaks of me,
Christ in every eye that sees me,
Christ in every ear that hears me.
I arise today
Through a mighty strength, the invocation of the Trinity,
Through belief in the threeness,
Through confession of the oneness
of the Creator of creation.

Prayer of John Henry Newman[3]
May the Lord support us all the day long,
Till the shades lengthen and the evening comes,
and the busy world is hushed, and the fever of life is over,
and our work is done.
Then in his mercy may he give us a safe lodging,
and holy rest, and peace at the last.

Amen.

PRAISE AND ADORATION

Prayers of praise can help you lift your thoughts beyond the concerns that surround you, focus on the meaning of what you do, or see the events of your life as being connected to and part of God's plan. You may benefit from adding spontaneous prayers of thanksgiving, creating a litany of the things for which you are grateful, or using the following prayers both to praise God and to contemplate the wonder of his glory and the beauty of his creation. You might use the following prayers for a short time of private prayer at the beginning or end of the day.

The Divine Praises

Blessed be God.
Blessed be his Holy Name.
Blessed be Jesus Christ, true God and true man.
Blessed be the Name of Jesus.
Blessed be His Most Sacred Heart.
Blessed be His Most Precious Blood.
Blessed be Jesus in the Most Holy Sacrament of the Altar.
Blessed be the Holy Spirit, the Paraclete.
Blessed be the great Mother of God, Mary most holy.
Blessed be her holy and Immaculate Conception.
Blessed be her glorious Assumption.
Blessed be the name of Mary, Virgin and Mother.
Blessed be Saint Joseph, her most chaste spouse.

Blessed be God in his angels and in his saints. Amen.

From the Sequence at Pentecost[4]
Come, Holy Spirit, come!
And from your celestial home
Shed a ray of light divine!

Come, Father of the poor!
Come, source of all our store!
Come, within our bosoms shine.

You, of comforters the best;
You, the soul's most welcome guest;
Sweet refreshment here below;

In our labor, rest most sweet;
Grateful coolness in the heat;
Solace in the midst of woe.

O most blessed Light divine,
Shine within these hearts of yours,
And our inmost being fill!

Canticle of the Sun[5]

Most high, all-powerful, all good, Lord!
All praise is yours, all glory, all honour
And all blessing.

To you alone, Most High, do they belong.
No mortal lips are worthy
To pronounce your name.

All praise be yours, my Lord, through all that you have made,
And first my lord Brother Sun,
Who brings the day; and light you give to us through him.

How beautiful is he, how radiant in all his splendour!
Of you, Most High, he bears the likeness.

All praise be yours my Lord, through Brothers Wind and Air,
And fair and stormy, all the weather's moods,
By which you cherish all that you have made.

All praise be yours, my Lord, through Sister Water,
So useful, lowly, precious and pure.

All praise be yours, my Lord, through Brother Fire,
Through whom you brighten up the night.

How beautiful is he, how gay! Full of power and strength.

All praise be yours my Lord, through Sister Earth, our mother
Who feeds us in her sovereignty and produces
Various fruits with colored flowers and herbs.

All praise be yours, my Lord, through those who grant pardon.
For love of you; through those who endure
Sickness and trial.

Happy those who endure in peace,
By you, Most High, they will be crowned.

All praise be yours, my Lord, through Sister Death,
From whose embrace no mortal can escape.
Woe to those who die in mortal sin!
Happy those She finds doing your will!
The second death can do no harm to them.

Praise and bless my Lord, and give him thanks,

And serve him with great humility.

Prayer of St. Teresa of Ávila[6]

Let nothing disturb you,
Let nothing frighten you,
All things are passing away:
God never changes.
Patience obtains all things
Whoever has God lacks nothing;
God alone suffices.

IV

The Holy Rosary

The Holy Rosary is the quintessential prayer to our Lady. As a single person, I prayed it daily. As a married woman, it felt difficult to commit to the necessary time. As a mother it felt nearly impossible to focus. Yet I know this prayer remains, since its popularization in the twelfth century, one of the greatest prayers we can pray. It combines the engagement of our senses through the use of rosary beads and our intellect through the meditation on the mysteries. The *Catechism of the Catholic Church* states: "Meditation is above all a quest. The mind seeks to understand the why and how behind the Christian life, in order to adhere and respond to what the Lord is asking" (2705).

In this quest, our feet follow the God-man's footprints in his journey from the Incarnation to the Coronation of Mary. We explore not only salvation events, but the intimacies and intricacies of the most glorious and unexpected mother-child relationship in history. We anticipate "what no eye has seen, nor ear heard, nor the heart of man conceived, what God has prepared for those who love him" (1 Cor 2:9).

As a mother and mentor, Mary seeks to show us the way of her motherhood, a way of total abandonment to God, a way of surrendering one's plans, of active receptivity through the choice to hear the word of God and keep it (see Lk 11:28).

As my own motherhood has continued, I have found the truth in the words of the *Catechism*, "One cannot always meditate, but one can always enter into inner prayer, independently of the conditions of health, work, or emotional state. The heart is the place of this quest and encounter, in poverty and in faith" (2710).

Whatever your current state, I invite you to do the same in your search for peace. The following meditations on the mysteries of the Rosary use Scripture passages and paintings depicting the events. Consider what you see and hear, and ask the Lord to show you what he has in store for you as it relates to your pregnancy and your search for peace.

The Joyful Mysteries

THE FIRST JOYFUL MYSTERY:
The Annunciation

Read

In the sixth month the angel Gabriel was sent from God
to a city of Galilee named Nazareth, to a virgin betrothed
to a man whose name was Joseph, of the house of David;
and the virgin's name was Mary. And he came to her and
said, "Hail, full of grace, the Lord is with you!" But she
was greatly troubled at the saying, and considered in her
mind what sort of greeting this might be. And the angel
said to her, "Do not be afraid, Mary, for you have found
favor with God. And behold, you will conceive in your
womb and bear a son, and you shall call his name Jesus.
He will be great, and will be called the Son of

the Most High;
and the Lord God will give to him the throne of

his father David,
and he will reign over the house of Jacob for
ever;
and of his kingdom there will be no end."
And Mary said to the angel, "How can this be, since I
have no husband?" And the angel said to her,
"The Holy Spirit will come upon you,
and the power of the Most High
will overshadow you;
therefore the child to be born will be called
holy,
the Son of God.
And behold, your kinswoman Elizabeth in her old age
has also conceived a son; and this is the sixth month
with her who was called barren. For with God nothing
will be impossible." And Mary said, "Behold, I am the
handmaid of the Lord; let it be to me according to your
word." And the angel departed from her. (Luke 1:26–36)

Reflect

What we see:

Mary hears the announcement. Her widened eyes take in the news. Her hands clasp tightly together, soon to open once more, reflecting her openness to God's will.

Facing the angel Gabriel's news, her world transforms. While the emotions peak and dip and swirl around her heart, her mind processes the news. If the announcement elated her, if it frightened her, if she scrambled to understand how it could be, none of those emotions altered her *fiat*.

Emotions are passions that arise in us. They happen to us. They fluctuate. Tanner's *The Annunciation* does not show Mary in unflappable serenity. Rather, we see her taking in the angel's appearance and news.

The passion arises, but then the will decides: "What will I do with this information?"

What we hear:
She steps past the emotions and, with her will, accepts God's hand. "Let it be to me according to your word," she says.

Pray
I can plan and hope, but I cannot know for sure what lies ahead for this pregnancy, my child, or me. Like Mary, help me to pray: "According to thy will, O God."

THE SECOND JOYFUL MYSTERY:
The Visitation

Read

In those days Mary arose and went with haste into the hill country, to a city of Judah, and she entered the house of Zechariah and greeted Elizabeth. And when Elizabeth heard the greeting of Mary, the child leaped in her womb; and Elizabeth was filled with the Holy Spirit and she exclaimed with a loud cry, "Blessed are you among women, and blessed is the fruit of your womb! And why is this granted me, that the mother of my Lord should come to me? For behold, when the voice of your greeting came to my ears, the child in my womb leaped for joy. And blessed is she who believed that there would be a fulfilment of what was spoken to her from the Lord." And Mary said,

"My soul magnifies the Lord,
and my spirit rejoices in God my Savior,
for he has regarded the low estate of his
    handmaiden.
For behold, henceforth all generations will call
    me blessed;
for he who is mighty has done great things for
    me,
and holy is his name.

And his mercy is on those who fear him
from generation to generation.
He has shown strength with his arm,
he has scattered the proud in the imagination
    of their hearts,
he has put down the mighty from their
    thrones,
and exalted those of low degree;
he has filled the hungry with good things,
and the rich he has sent empty away.
He has helped his servant Israel,
in remembrance of his mercy,
as he spoke to our fathers,
to Abraham and to his posterity for ever."
And Mary remained with her about three months,
and returned to her home. (Luke 1:39–56)

Reflect

What we see:

Elizabeth perceives a leap within her. Her hand presses down, moving across her belly to locate her son's movement. Lifting her hands, she embraces her cousin. Under her heart, the baby boy jumps. His movement draws her deeper into her awareness of his inexplicable existence — his personality, his personhood — and into the Presence of God. The motion recalls to her the incredible gift of the conception of the Forerunner of Christ, the depth of God's love, and his desire for her to participate in his plan. Through his movement, the unborn John communicates to her. Through her child, God speaks to her.

What does she hear? What will she say?

In Pontormo's *Visitation*, Elizabeth greets her cousin Mary with a knowing look. Mary returns her gaze. These women share a secret. In their unity, they attest to something greater than this world.

What we hear:

Elizabeth exclaims, "And blessed is she who believed that there would be a fulfilment of what was spoken to her from the Lord" (Lk 1:45). Mary is blessed among women for this faith. Christ promises that we too shall be blessed when we hear the word of God and keep it (see Lk 11:28).

Pray

My body mirrors the experience of Mary and Elizabeth. There is greatness here beyond my own plans. I will choose to believe in the promises of God. Mary, teach me to remember and to praise: "For he who is mighty has done great things for me" (Lk 1:49).

THE THIRD JOYFUL MYSTERY:
The Nativity of Christ Our Lord

Read

And Joseph also went up from Galilee, from the city of Nazareth, to Judea, to the city of David, which is called Bethlehem, because he was of the house and lineage of David, to be enrolled with Mary his betrothed, who was with child. And while they were there, the time came for her to be delivered. And she gave birth to her first-born son and wrapped him in swaddling cloths, and laid him in a manger, because there was no place for them in the inn.

And in that region there were shepherds out in the field, keeping watch over their flock by night. And an angel of the Lord appeared to them, and the glory of the Lord shone around them, and they were filled with fear. And the angel said to them, "Be not afraid; for behold, I bring you good news of a great joy which will come to all the people; for to you is born this day in the city of David a Savior, who is Christ the Lord. And this will be a sign for you: You will find a baby wrapped in swaddling cloths and lying in a manger." And suddenly there was with the angel a multitude of the heavenly host praising God and saying,

"Glory to God in the highest,
and on earth peace among men with whom he
is pleased!"

When the angels went away from them into heaven,
the shepherds said to one another, "Let us go over to
Bethlehem and see this thing that has happened, which
the Lord has made known to us." And they went with
haste, and found Mary and Joseph, and the baby lying in
a manger. And when they saw it they made known the
saying which had been told them concerning this child;
and all who heard it wondered at what the shepherds
told them. But Mary kept all these things, pondering
them in her heart. And the shepherds returned, glorify-
ing and praising God for all they had heard and seen, as
it had been told them. (Luke 2:4–20)

Reflect

What we see:

In *The Adoration of the Shepherds* by Christian Wilhelm Ernst
Dietrich, strangers enter the peaceful scene on their knees. Joseph extends his arms in surprise. Mary's serenity emanates
from her as she kneels before her Son, her face turned, sharing
that light with the shepherds, who are offering effusive praise.

In these early years, the child's story is intimately bound
together with his mother's story. She introduces us to him and

helps us to see him for the king that he is.

John Paul II explains:

> No one has ever devoted himself to the contemplation of the face of Christ as faithfully as Mary. The eyes of her heart already turned to him at the Annunciation, when she conceived him by the power of the Holy Spirit. In the months that followed she began to sense his presence and to picture his features. When at last she gave birth to him in Bethlehem, her eyes were able to gaze tenderly on the face of her Son, as she "wrapped him in swaddling cloths, and laid him in a manger."[1]

What we hear:

"Mary kept all these things, pondering them in her heart" (Lk 1:19). Mary sits, setting aside the concerns, the questions, the world's judgment, focusing her heart on her Son, seeing him, knowing him, loving him. As our love and knowledge grow, the better can we embrace the will of God, no matter how challenging. His will becomes our will.

Pray

Life may not be as I plan it. Reality is more outside my jurisdiction than I prefer. Lord, help me to know you, to open my heart as your events unfold, and to sing along with the angels at my child's birth: "Glory to God in the highest, and on earth peace among men with whom he is pleased!" (Lk 2:14).

THE FOURTH JOYFUL MYSTERY:
The Presentation of Jesus in the Temple

Read

And at the end of eight days, when he was circumcised, he was called Jesus, the name given by the angel before he was conceived in the womb.

And when the time came for their purification according to the law of Moses, they brought him up to Jerusalem to present him to the Lord (as it is written in the law of the Lord, "Every male that opens the womb shall be called holy to the Lord") and to offer a sacrifice according to what is said in the law of the Lord, "a pair of turtledoves, or two young pigeons." Now there was a man in Jerusalem, whose name was Simeon, and this man was righteous and devout, awaiting for the consolation of Israel, and the Holy Spirit was upon him. And it had been revealed to him by the Holy Spirit that he should not see death before he had seen the Lord's Christ. And inspired by the Spirit he came into the temple; and when the parents brought in the child Jesus, to act according to the custom of the law, he took him up in his arms and blessed God and said,

"Lord, now let your servant depart in peace,

according to your word;
for my eyes have seen your salvation
which you have prepared in the presence of all
        peoples,
a light for revelation to the Gentiles,
and for glory to your people Israel."
And his father and his mother marveled at what was
said about him; and Simeon blessed them and said
to Mary his mother,
"Behold, this child is set for the fall and rising
        of many in Israel,
and for a sign that is spoken against
(and a sword will pierce through your own soul
        also),
that thoughts out of many hearts may be
        revealed." (Luke 2:21–35)

Reflect

What we see:

The Mother of God wants to keep her son safe. She desires to keep him near her, to protect him, love him, and shield him from the evil of the world. Simeon approaches her with the eyes of an old man who sees beyond the veil. In *Simeon's Song of Praise* Rembrandt bathes the Holy Family in light. Embracing the Christ, the Light of the World, Simeon pierces the mystery of the boy he takes into his arms. Breathless, he lifts his misty eyes to the Almighty.

Life is built of longing, a sense of the "not yet." Mary's youthful hands hold close the vision shared with her. In light of this seemingly coincidental encounter, she perceives God's plan. It will be fulfilled, surpassing all she can imagine.

What we hear:

"Now there was a man in Jerusalem, whose name was Simeon, and this man was righteous and devout, awaiting for the consolation of Israel" (Lk 2:25). Simeon waits for not just the fulfillment of the prophecies, but the consolation of his people. Moments of consolation will come to us, when God offers us reassurance. Will we hold those moments in our hearts as signs of his fidelity?

Pray

At each doctor's appointment, through a machine, I encounter the child I cannot yet see or touch. I hear the heartbeat echo through the doppler speaker or see the body squirm across the grainy screen. I hold my breath waiting while the doctor or nurse locates these signs of life. Then suddenly on the monitor, there is my child! In this vision, I grasp the peace of my child's revelation. Lord, may I hold this moment and walk forward in peace.

THE FIFTH JOYFUL MYSTERY:
The Finding of Jesus in the Temple

Read

And the child grew and became strong, filled with wisdom; and the favor of God was upon him.

Now his parents went to Jerusalem every year at the feast of the Passover. And when he was twelve years old, they went up according to custom; and when the feast was ended, as they were returning, the boy Jesus stayed behind in Jerusalem. His parents did not know it, but supposing him to be in the company they went a day's journey, and they sought him among their kinsfolk and acquaintances; and when they did not find him, they returned to Jerusalem, seeking him. After three days they found him in the temple, sitting among the teachers, listening to them and asking them questions; and all who heard him were amazed at his understanding and his answers. And when they saw him they were astonished; and his mother said to him, "Son, why have you treated us so? Behold, your father and I have been looking for you anxiously." And he said to them, "How is it that you sought me? Did you not know that I must be in my Father's house?" And they did not understand the saying which he spoke to them. And he went down with them and came to Nazareth, and was obedient to them; and his mother kept all these things in her heart.

And Jesus increased in wisdom and in stature, and in favor with God and man. (Luke 2:40–52)

Reflect

What we see:

In the background of this painting, *Christ among the Doctors* by Vasily Polenov, almost beyond view, Mary discovers her son, whom she has sought frantically. An adolescent Jesus attends to the teacher's words, leaning forward, eyes wide open, devouring the knowledge and ideas expounded before him. They are amazed at his understanding.

The Christ does not belong to the Virgin. Rather, he is entrusted to her. She pauses, seeing her Son begin his transition beyond his identity as the carpenter's Son, beyond the family who raised him, to his mission in the wider world.

What we hear:

Mary asks with an open heart and mind, desiring to know, "Son, why have you treated us so? Behold, your father and I have been looking for you anxiously" (Lk 2:48). She wants to understand. Seeking answers does not point to a lack of faith when we seek with a willingness to receive an answer we may not understand. Her Son has grown beyond her, his story grows more independent from hers, and she desires to learn about this part of him.

Pray
Reflecting on the milestones of pregnancy: first trimester, first kick, the twenty-week anatomy scan, full term at forty weeks, and delivery. I see each milestone is full of possibility and so beyond my control. A person grows at his or her own pace. I pause, as Our Lady did, to behold for a moment this individual who defies all my expectations, to whom I incline my ear and loosen my resolutions in order to explore God's plan. Help me to hold all this in my heart.

The Luminous Mysteries

THE FIRST LUMINOUS MYSTERY:
The Baptism of Jesus in the Jordan

Read

> Then Jesus came from Galilee to the Jordan to John, to be baptized by him. John would have prevented him, saying, "I need to be baptized by you, and do you come to me?" But Jesus answered him, "Let it be so now; for thus it is fitting for us to fulfil all righteousness." Then he consented. And when Jesus was baptized, he went up immediately from the water, and behold, the heavens were opened and he saw the Spirit of God descending like a dove, and alighting on him; and behold, a voice from heaven, saying, "This is my beloved Son, with whom I am well pleased." (Matthew 3:13–17)

After this Jesus and his disciples went into the land of

Judea; there he remained with them and baptized. John also was baptizing at Aenon near Salim, because there was much water there; and people came and were baptized. For John had not yet been put in prison.

Now a discussion arose between John's disciples and a Jew over purifying. And they came to John, and said to him, "Rabbi, he who was with you beyond the Jordan, to whom you bore witness, here he is, baptizing, and all are going to him." John answered, "No one can receive anything except what is given him from heaven. You yourselves bear me witness, that I said, I am not the Christ, but I have been sent before him. He who has the bride is the bridegroom; the friend of the bridegroom, who stands and hears him, rejoices greatly at the bridegroom's voice; therefore this joy of mine is now full. He must increase, but I must decrease." (John 3:22–30)

Reflect

What we see:

In *The Baptism of Christ* by Giotto, the sky opens reveal a glimpse into the Divine Trinity: Father, Son, and Holy Spirit. A voice from heaven speaks, identifying his Word as his Son. The Spirit hovers over the waters and descends like a dove on Jesus, declaring the unity between the Father and the Son.

The angels wait to receive the naked Christ. Though without sin, he shows us the way to rebirth and new life. The angels receive him. The Trinity affirms him. For this brief moment, we glimpse the Glory of the Incarnate Word.

What we hear:

The Baptist is both the sign and the symbol: the active player and yet the one whose image fades before the bright Messianic revelation. The wild man of the desert lays the foundation, draws sinners to the water, and exhorts them to repent. John points to Christ. Jesus will increase and John will decrease (see Jn 3:30).

These actions of the Baptist facilitate this great revelation during the Baptism of Christ. After acting as instrument for this moment, John declares, "He must increase, but I must decrease" (Jn 3:30).

Pray

New life begins in pregnancy: my child's life, but also a new life in me. I have changed. To me is revealed a mystery greater than myself. While still fully myself, I feel within me that call: "He must increase, but I must decrease" (Jn 3:30). May I find in this pregnancy the opportunity to give of myself, now and in the future, to help this child become the person it is called to be.

THE SECOND LUMINOUS MYSTERY:
The Wedding at Cana

Read

On the third day there was a marriage at Cana in Galilee, and the mother of Jesus was there; Jesus also was invited to the marriage, with his disciples. When the wine failed, the mother of Jesus said to him, "They have no wine." And Jesus said to her, "O woman, what have you to do with me? My hour has not yet come." His mother said to the servants, "Do whatever he tells you." Now six stone jars were standing there, for the Jewish rites of purification, each holding twenty or thirty gallons. Jesus said to them, "Fill the jars with water." And they filled them up to the brim. He said to them, "Now draw some out, and take it to the steward of the feast." So they took it. When the steward of the feast tasted the water now become wine, and did not know where it came from (though the servants who had drawn the water knew), the steward of the feast called the bridegroom and said to him, "Every man serves the good wine first; and when men have drunk freely, then the poor wine; but you have kept the good wine until now." This, the first of his signs, Jesus did at Cana in Galilee, and manifested his glory; and his disciples believed in him. (John 2:1–11)

Reflect

What we see:

Discreetly, Our Lady approaches him. Discreetly, he directs the servants. And in Tintoretto's *Marriage at Cana*, Mary and Jesus sit discreetly while the action unfolds around them. They have done all that needed to be done. The Star of the Sea has interceded as a vessel, through which the Savior has manifested himself to the world in this first miracle. Jesus acts. Now Tintoretto paints the moment following: the servants filling the jugs, a servant serving a glass, the head steward amazed.

What we hear:

Our Lady of Good Counsel observes and acts. She observes to her son, "They have no wine" (Jn 2:3). Jesus has not yet begun his public ministry — but if he does what his mother appears to be asking him to do, he will embark on a new journey, one that takes him from the quiet life of home, his mother, and work to send him traveling from village to village with disciples, performing more miracles. Scripture does not tell us what Mary anticipates or understands, but we know she stored much in her heart. She sees a need. She knows her Son can fill that need. She acts.

Pray

My pregnancy now lays the groundwork for this kind of anticipation, when a mother can perceive so beautifully the needs around her and how her children are particular gifts to serve those needs. Lord, help me to know this child of mine!

THE THIRD LUMINOUS MYSTERY
The Proclamation of the Kingdom of God

Read

> Now as they went on their way, he entered a village; and a woman named Martha received him into her house. And she had a sister called Mary, who sat at the Lord's feet and listened to his teaching. But Martha was distracted with much serving; and she went to him and said, "Lord, do you not care that my sister has left me to serve alone? Tell her then to help me." But the Lord answered her, "Martha, Martha, you are anxious and troubled about many things; one thing is needful. Mary has chosen the good portion, which shall not be taken away from her." (Luke 10:38–42)

> [Another time,] when Jesus came, he found that Lazarus had already been in the tomb four days. Bethany was near Jerusalem, about two miles off, and many of the Jews had come to Martha and Mary to console them concerning their brother. When Martha heard that Jesus was coming, she went and met him, while Mary sat in the house. Martha said to Jesus, "Lord, if you had been here, my brother would not have died. And even now I know that whatever you ask from God, God

will give you." Jesus said to her, "Your brother will rise again." Martha said to him, "I know that he will rise again in the resurrection at the last day." Jesus said to her, "I am the resurrection and the life; he who believes in me, though he die, yet shall he live, and whoever lives and believes in me shall never die. Do you believe this?" She said to him, "Yes, Lord; I believe that you are the Christ, the Son of God, he who is coming into the world." (John 11:17–27)

Reflect

What we see:

In *Christ at the Home of Mary and Martha* by Henry Ossawa Tanner, Christ shares a meal with Martha and Mary at some point during his friendship with them. Perhaps the painter is depicting that famous conversation in which Christ says, "Martha, Martha, you are anxious and troubled about many things" (Lk 10:41). Or the painter could have been depicting one of many other meals. Martha stands with a plate in hand while Mary sits with Christ at the table. He gestures to Mary.

What we hear:

In Christ's response, he hears and receives the heart of Martha. "You are anxious" (Lk 10:41). He does not reject her complaints. Rather, he reads her heart. Later, at her brother's death, while

Mary sits at the tomb and grieves, Martha goes to Christ. Again, she speaks forthrightly. "Lord, if you had been here, my brother would not have died" (Jn 11:42). This time, rather than offering emotional understanding and sage advice, the Messiah acts. Jesus fixes the problem. He heals the wound. He raises the dead.

Pray
Lord, I know that you love me. Through the honesty of Martha, you saw the state of her heart, and you spoke to her in her need. Please hear my concerns (name them). Please hear me with understanding, consolation, correction, or intervention, according to your will, O God.

THE FOURTH LUMINOUS MYSTERY:
The Transfiguration

Read

> And after six days Jesus took with him Peter and James and John, and led them up a high mountain apart by themselves; and he was transfigured before them, and his garments became glistening, intensely white, as no fuller on earth could bleach them. And there appeared to them Elijah with Moses; and they were talking to Jesus. And Peter said to Jesus, "Master, it is well that we are here; let us make three booths, one for you and one for Moses and one for Elijah." For he did not know what to say, for they were exceedingly afraid. And a cloud overshadowed them, and a voice came out from the cloud, "This is my beloved Son; listen to him." And suddenly looking around they no longer saw any one with them but Jesus only. (Mark 9:2–8)

Reflect

What we see:

Ultimately, Jesus is familiar to us because of his descent, in which he lowered himself to become one of us though he is higher than the angels (see Heb 1:4). Christ reveals the full measure of who he is — the Son of God — to those who love him most, to those whom he chooses.

What we hear:
Pope St. John Paul II wrote:

> The mystery of light par excellence is the Transfiguration, traditionally believed to have taken place on Mount Tabor. The glory of the Godhead shines forth from the face of Christ as the Father commands the astonished Apostles to "listen to him" (cf. Lk 9:35 and parallels) and to prepare to experience with him the agony of the Passion, so as to come with him to the joy of the Resurrection and a life transfigured by the Holy Spirit.[2]

Pray
You show me your glory in the Transfiguration. This epiphany bolstered the disciples through the shock and misery during the arrest, scourging, and crucifixion. They held your figure before their eyes and hearts when they no longer recognized you in your agony. This vision fulfilled the meaning of the blood and tears poured out when your time had arrived. As I labor through this time of waiting, pain, and trial, may the vision of expectant joy in cradling my baby sustain me.

THE FIFTH LUMINOUS MYSTERY:
The Institution of the Eucharist

Read

And when the hour came, he sat at table, and the apostles with him. And he said to them, "I have earnestly desired to eat this Passover with you before I suffer; for I tell you I shall not eat it until it is fulfilled in the kingdom of God." And he took a chalice, and when he had given thanks he said, "Take this, and divide it among yourselves; for I tell you that from now on I shall not drink of the fruit of the vine until the kingdom of God comes." And he took bread, and when he had given thanks he broke it and gave it to them, saying, "This is my body which is given for you. Do this in remembrance of me." And likewise the chalice after supper, saying, "This chalice which is poured out for you is the new covenant in my blood." (Luke 22:14–20)

Jesus said to them, "I am the bread of life; he who comes to me shall not hunger, and he who believes in me shall never thirst. But I said to you that you have seen me and yet do not believe. All that the Father gives me will come to me; and him who comes to me I will not cast out. For I have come down from heaven, not to do my own will,

but the will of him who sent me; and this is the will of him who sent me, that I should lose nothing of all that he has given me, but raise it up at the last day. For this is the will of my Father, that every one who sees the Son and believes in him should have eternal life; and I will raise him up at the last day."

"I am the living bread which came down from heaven; if any one eats of this bread, he will live for ever; and the bread which I shall give for the life of the world is my flesh." (John 6:35–40, 51)

Reflect

What we see:

The most ordinary things hold extraordinary wonders. The offerings look like bread and wine: simple, unaltered, like any wheat bread and grape wine. Some reject them, but others understand that this is the only way to eternal life. In *Eucharist* by Nicolas Poussin, we see the apostles' hands raised in amazement. Some reach to eat, and one exits quietly into the darkness.

What we hear:

Christ is the priest. He says, "This cup which is poured out for you is the new covenant in my blood" (Lk 22:20). As priest, he offers the sacrifice in atonement.

Pray

I participate in the priesthood as a baptized woman: not as the ordained priests do, but in a uniquely feminine way, in my motherhood. Pregnancy can seem common, ordinary, and bodily. Yet it reaches into the deepest mystery. Lord, I offer up my pain and concerns, and I trust that you will transform my offering. I offer this suffering as a prayer for my child.

The Sorrowful Mysteries

THE FIRST SORROWFUL MYSTERY:
The Agony in the Garden

Read

"O Jerusalem, Jerusalem, killing the prophets and stoning those who are sent to you! How often would I have gathered your children together as a hen gathers her brood under her wings, and you would not!"

Then Jesus went with them to a place called Gethsemane, and he said to his disciples, "Sit here, while I go over there and pray." And taking with him Peter and the two sons of Zebedee, he began to be sorrowful and troubled. Then he said to them, "My soul is very sorrowful, even to death; remain here, and watch with me." And going a little farther he fell on his face and prayed, "My Father, if it be possible, let this chalice pass from me; nevertheless, not as I will, but as you will." (Matthew 23:37; 26:36–39)

> And there appeared to him an angel from heaven, strengthening him. And being in an agony he prayed more earnestly; and his sweat became like great drops of blood falling down upon the ground. And when he rose from prayer, he came to the disciples and found them sleeping for sorrow, and he said to them, "Why do you sleep? Rise and pray that you may not enter into temptation" (Lk 22:43–46).

Reflect

What we see:

An angel appears to comfort him. In *The Agony in the Garden*, Rembrandt illustrates a Christ who has not succumbed to grief but who faces the angel, stretching out his hand to reciprocate the angel's comforting touch. The Suffering Servant "encounters all the temptations and confronts all the sins of humanity."[3]

He looks ahead and sees the hardship that lies before him. According to John Paul II, "This 'Yes' of Christ reverses the 'No' of our first parents in the Garden of Eden."[4] He looks ahead but still accepts the angel's compassion. The angel turns to the Master, communicates with him, sees his sorrow, face-to-face.

In the sketch's background, the guards approach to arrest him. Off to the side, the disciples sleep. Jesus faces the temptation and triumphs by continuing to pray.

What we hear:

He prepares his heart. The Son awaits his Father's will. He prays, "Nevertheless, not as I will, but as you will" (Mt 26:39).

Pray

Lord, the sorrowful mysteries invite us to think about suffering very directly. Rather than run, avoid, or sleep, as the apostles responded to your ordeal, help me to keep my companions at my side. Help me to turn toward my guardian angel. I entrust my future to you and the future of my child.

THE SECOND SORROWFUL MYSTERY:
The Scourging at the Pillar

Read

> Jesus answered, "My kingship is not of this world; if my kingship were of this world, my servants would fight, that I might not be handed over to the Jews; but my kingship is not from the world." Pilate said to him, "So you are a king?" Jesus answered, "You say that I am a king. For this I was born, and for this I have come into the world, to bear witness to the truth. Every one who is of the truth hears my voice." Pilate said to him, "What is truth?"
>
> Then Pilate took Jesus and scourged him. (John 18:36–38; 19:1)

Reflect

What we see:

The Son of David stands, his hands tied, his head bowed, as blood runs down his hair, his head, and his back, staining the pavement beneath him. He is exposed, restrained, torn open, abused. The foolish Herod and the fearful Pilate drive the narrative. Whatever they understand, it does not include suffering's mystery. They question his motives, his decisions, and his silence. Why should he endure it?

In each episode of this narrative, each man's judgment is

flung upon the Christ. He accedes to their condemnation. The time of preparation is over. Each moment is an act of submission, the next more painful than the last.

What we hear:
For this, he was born. In *Gaudium et Spes*, we read, "Man ... cannot fully find himself except through a sincere gift of himself."[5] For this we are born.

So Christ was scourged leading up to the crucifixion. His gift to us was not a single offering in a single moment, but rather contained numerous little offerings from his interactions, his healings, his forgiveness, his remonstrances, and now, physically, concretely, his passion.

Pray
As I move through pregnancy, Lord, so let me see it myself. These little acts of love, the appointments, the sleeplessness, all of it, preparing my heart not just for the moment of delivery, but for the new life of my child.

THE THIRD SORROWFUL MYSTERY:
The Crowning with Thorns

Read

> And the soldiers plaited a crown of thorns, and put it on his head, and clothed him in a purple robe; they came up to him, saying, "Hail, King of the Jews!" and struck him with their hands. Pilate went out again, and said to them, "Behold, I am bringing him out to you, that you may know that I find no crime in him." So Jesus came out, wearing the crown of thorns and the purple robe. Pilate said to them, "Here is the man!" (John 19:2–5)

Reflect

What we see:

"Here is the man," Pilate says. But this is God! Here is the Christ, the Word who spoke and brought everything into being, Light from Light, True God from True God, begotten not made, reduced to a mockery. In *Christ Crowned with Thorns* by Maerten van Heemskerck, we see the contorted faces of his abusers reveling while Christ sits suffering, but at peace.

What we hear:

Christ, the Word of God, permits the suffering and abuse to proceed. His body will be prodded and displayed, but his dignity

remains. He knows who he is and from whence he comes. This is the Father's beloved Son, and no indignity can diminish that.

Pray

How strange to see how my bodily changes in pregnancy, and how my body will change when my time to deliver comes. Without a drop of romance, in the sweat, in the vulnerability, in the pain, my child will come. Help me to hold in my heart that through it all, my dignity remains, beauty remains, and peace can also remain.

THE FOURTH SORROWFUL MYSTERY:
The Way of the Cross

Read

> Then Jesus told his disciples, "If any man would come after me, let him deny himself and take up his cross and follow me. For whoever would save his life will lose it, and whoever loses his life for my sake will find it. For what will it profit a man, if he gains the whole world and forfeits his life? Or what shall a man give in return for his life? For the Son of man is to come with his angels in the glory of his Father, and then he will repay every man for what he has done. Truly, I say to you, there are some standing here who will not taste death before they see the Son of man coming in his kingdom." (Matthew 16:24–28)

> So they took Jesus, and he went out, bearing his own cross, to the place called the place of a skull, which is called in Hebrew Golgotha. (John 19:17)

Reflect

What we see:

Step by step it begins. One agonizing stride after another. With his eyes lifted to the Father, the passion punishes the Son of

God with waves of pain. Jesus endures. He falls. He gets up. He is helped. Some see his sorrow. Some comfort him. Others are oblivious to the grace with which the Son of Man endures as he pours out his body and blood for the new life of the children of God. El Greco shows us the Redeemer lifting his eyes to heaven in *Christ Carrying the Cross*. With his serenity, knowledge of the Father, the plan of salvation, the purpose of this trial bears him forward.

What we hear:
"If any man would come after me, let him deny himself and take up his cross and follow me" (Jn 16:24). Carrying the cross in peace does not mean it no longer hurts. The goal of the battle is to maintain peace amid trial, even torment.[6] One agonizing step at a time.

Pray
When the contractions come, help me face each one on its own, each wave as it rises and falls. May I accept the comfort that comes, as you did when you carried your cross. There will be moments of rest, even as my body prepares for the final moment of delivery. Christ, you carried you cross. I do not have to carry mine alone.

THE FIFTH SORROWFUL MYSTERY:
THE CRUCIFIXION

Read

But standing by the cross of Jesus were his mother, and his mother's sister, Mary the wife of Clopas, and Mary Magdalene. When Jesus saw his mother, and the disciple whom he loved standing near, he said to his mother, "Woman, behold, your son!" Then he said to the disciple, "Behold, your mother!" And from that hour the disciple took her to his own home.

After this Jesus, knowing that all was now finished, said (to fulfil the Scripture), "I thirst." A bowl full of vinegar stood there; so they put a sponge full of the vinegar on hyssop and held it to his mouth. (John 19:25–29)

It was now about the sixth hour, and there was darkness over the whole land until the ninth hour, while the sun's light failed; and the curtain of the temple was torn in two. Then Jesus, crying with a loud voice, said, "Father, into your hands I commit my spirit!" And having said this he breathed his last. (Luke 23:44–46)

Reflect

What we see:

In *Crucifixion* by Franz Stuck, Mary faints at that great release of power and her Son's death. She has watched and waited, walked close at hand. There is nothing more to be done, but to rest and anticipate the prophecy's fulfillment.

What we hear:

With a loud cry, the Son of Man gives up his spirit. At that moment, our salvation is at hand. He descends to the dead to release those who waited in the sleep of righteousness. They are caught up into the clouds to meet the Lord. In a clamor the dead rise from their graves. The earth shakes, the veil is torn, the spirit goes out, and his lifeblood is released.

Pray

With a cry and a push, my baby will be born. Exhausted, I will fall back on the pillows in a daze as they return my newborn to me. However those moments may look, even if different than I anticipate, I can pray. I pray that as I face whatever uncertainty will come, I will rest in you, my God.

The Glorious Mysteries

THE FIRST GLORIOUS MYSTERY:
The Resurrection of Jesus from the Dead

Read

Now after the sabbath, toward the dawn of the first day
of the week, Mary Magdalene and the other Mary went
to see the tomb. And behold, there was a great earth-
quake; for an angel of the Lord descended from heaven
and came and rolled back the stone, and sat upon it. His
appearance was like lightning, and his clothing white as
snow. And for fear of him the guards trembled and became like dead men. But the angel said to the women,
"Do not be afraid; for I know that you seek Jesus who
was crucified. He is not here; for he has risen, as he
said. Come, see the place where he lay. Then go quickly
and tell his disciples that he has risen from the dead,
and behold, he is going before you to Galilee; there you

will see him. Behold, I have told you." So they departed quickly from the tomb with fear and great joy, and ran to tell his disciples. And behold, Jesus met them and said, "Hail!" And they came up and took hold of his feet and worshiped him. Then Jesus said to them, "Do not be afraid; go and tell my brethren to go to Galilee, and there they will see me." (Matthew 28:1–10)

Reflect

What we see:

They approach the tomb in grief. The women who witnessed Christ's crucifixion surround the entrance to fulfill the honor due to their Lord's body. With purpose and expectation, they draw near. Their world, already jolted to its core at their beloved's death, quakes as they behold God's messenger. In this moment we see them, daring to peer into the cave. The soldiers on guard flee, but those who come to serve with tenderness remain and receive the tidings. These women together recognize the Christ. While disciples hide in the Upper Room, the female cohort has been entrusted with the task to run to Galilee and proclaim the Good News.

What we hear:

"He is not here; for he has risen, as he said. Come, see the place where he lay" (Mt 28:6).

Pray

The looking, the waiting, the wondering are all intimately bound up with the mystery of pregnancy. Soon I will see my child, meet my child. Then, Lord, these moments of reflection will come into light. I pray I will better understand more deeply the meaning behind this search for peace. Like the women approaching the tomb, Lord, may my heart be open and ready to embrace the plans you have prepared for me.

THE SECOND GLORIOUS MYSTERY:
The Ascension of Jesus into Heaven

Read

So when they had come together, they asked him, "Lord, will you at this time restore the kingdom to Israel?" He said to them, "It is not for you to know times or seasons which the Father has fixed by his own authority. But you shall receive power when the Holy Spirit has come upon you; and you shall be my witnesses in Jerusalem and in all Judea and Samaria and to the end of the earth." And when he had said this, as they were looking on, he was lifted up, and a cloud took him out of their sight. And while they were gazing into heaven as he went, behold, two men stood by them in white robes, and said, "Men of Galilee, why do you stand looking into heaven? This Jesus, who was taken up from you into heaven, will come in the same way as you saw him go into heaven."

All these with one accord devoted themselves to prayer, together with the women and Mary the mother of Jesus, and with his brethren. (Acts 1:6–11, 14)

Reflect

What we see:

In a glorious, yet heartbreaking event, the Teacher leaves the apostles alone atop the hill. They had prophesies, explanations, and lessons to prepare them. But their friend has only just been restored to them, risen from the dead. Now they lose him again.

Why does Christ leave them? If he does not, the Comforter cannot come (see Jn 16:7). This Ascension must happen so that his word may be fulfilled. In this trust, they maintain peace.

What we hear:

> "It is not for you to know times or seasons which the Father has fixed by his own authority. But you shall receive power when the Holy Spirit has come upon you" (Acts 1:7–8).

Pray

Lord, embracing the holy offering of the present moment will not always give me answers. It is in hindsight that I more easily perceive your hand in all things. Why does it have to be this way?

Help me repeat the words when I struggle: that his plan may be fulfilled.

Lord, send me your Spirit, a Spirit of peace and understanding.

THE THIRD GLORIOUS MYSTERY:
Pentecost

Read

> When the day of Pentecost had come, they were all together in one place. And suddenly a sound came from heaven like the rush of a mighty wind, and it filled all the house where they were sitting. And there appeared to them tongues as of fire, distributed and resting on each one of them. And they were all filled with the Holy Spirit and began to speak in other tongues, as the Spirit gave them utterance. (Acts 2:1–4)

Reflect

What we see:

At the Ascension, the apostles gaped at the sky. Ten days later, in a mighty wind, all eyes fix on heaven above, as the Holy Spirit plummets with fire and magnificent light, filling their mouths with languages and prophecies.

What we hear:

The Father keeps his promise. Where once the apostles walked together, now they raise the dead; where once they prayed together, now they speak in tongues. The Holy Spirit dwells within us, transforming our actions into acts of God, the supernatural

consummating the natural. The Almighty dwells within us and will never leave us.

Pray

This majestic reality exists in the conception and birth of every child. Ordinary events become extraordinary as your Holy Spirit breathes life into my womb, infusing the body with a soul, unifying them to one being so that I possess not only my soul but I carry another's soul as well. My body holds a miracle. Help me hold this reality before me throughout this journey.

THE FOURTH GLORIOUS MYSTERY:
The Assumption of the Blessed Virgin Mary

Read

> For the Lord himself will descend from heaven with a cry of command, with the archangel's call, and with the sound of the trumpet of God. And the dead in Christ will rise first; then we who are alive, who are left, shall be caught up together with them in the clouds to meet the Lord in the air; and so we shall always be with the Lord. Therefore comfort one another with these words. (1 Thessalonians 4:16–18)

It was fitting that she, who had kept her virginity intact in childbirth, should keep her own body free from all corruption even after death. It was fitting that she, who had carried the Creator as a child at her breast, should dwell in the divine tabernacles. It was fitting that the spouse, whom the Father had taken to himself, should live in the divine mansions. It was fitting that she, who had seen her Son upon the cross and who had thereby received into her heart the sword of sorrow which she had escaped when giving birth to him, should look upon him as he sits with the Father. It was fitting that God's Mother should possess what belongs to her Son, and that she should be honored by every creature as the Mother and as the handmaid of God.[7]

Reflect

What we see:

From the tomb, the angels bear her to heaven. Her eyes gaze upward as she takes to the clouds, a symbol of the Presence of God. The Father, Son, and Holy Spirit assume Mary, body and soul, into heaven.

In her Immaculate Conception, the Mother of Jesus received the first fruits of her Son's sacrifice, freeing her from original sin. In the Assumption, he pledges that the dead shall rise.

Though her heart was pierced by a sword of sorrow, in the Assumption, God shows us that suffering is not the end.

What we read:

"Therefore comfort one another with these words" (1 Thes 4:18).

Pray

It is a strange privilege that allows me to carry a child, a privilege granted to many, but not all. Lord, help me to see that in this experience, through my body you show us a small example of this glorious Assumption. We meet suffering face to face that we might meet our little ones, whose souls will live for all eternity.

THE FIFTH GLORIOUS MYSTERY:
The Coronation of Mary Queen of Heaven and Earth

Read

> As he said this, a woman in the crowd raised her voice and said to him, "Blessed is the womb that bore you, and the breasts that you sucked!" But he said, "Blessed rather are those who hear the word of God and keep it!" (Luke 11:27–28)

> Do not fear what you are about to suffer. Behold, the devil is about to throw some of you into prison, that you may be tested, and for ten days you will have tribulation. Be faithful unto death, and I will give you the crown of life.
>
> And a great sign appeared in heaven, a woman clothed with the sun, with the moon under her feet, and on her head a crown of twelve stars. (Revelation 2:10; 12:1)

Reflect

What we see:

The woman's gift will not be overlooked by the Bridegroom. Jesus Christ crowns Mary Queen of Heaven and Earth, Queen of the Angels and Saints, the Theotokos, the God-bearer, the Throne of

God. Mary's life, prophesied before she was born, culminates in this heavenly moment. It exhibits to man and woman the path and the reward for our faithfulness to God.

What we hear:

> "Blessed rather are those who hear the word of God and keep it!" (Lk 11:28).

Pray

No mother is "just a mother." While I see the world glorify external action, I see in the Coronation that a mother's invisible majesty remains the vocation most honored by God among men. Her gift will be rewarded, as will the sacrifices of all who follow after her. O Lord, help me remember that I follow after the Virgin Mary in these steps of mine in pregnancy, and that I can follow after her spiritually in hearing your word and keeping it!

V

The Stations of the Cross

When we pray the Stations of the Cross, we ask the Lamb of God to allow us to accompany him on his way. Each station is a resting point, a transitional point, a point that invites us to pause and hold close to our hearts an aspect of Christ's journey in our meditation.

Our ability to be present during Mass may shift with pregnancy. The way we pray evolves as lung capacity diminishes. Kneeling is not the same as before, now that our belly pushes against the pew in front of us. Genuflecting or standing for long periods requires negotiation.

But each station here offers a meditation, a quest, whether our prayer includes the postures or whether we choose to sit and let thoughts do the moving for us.

The invitation stands.

In the *Stabat Mater*, we encounter Christ's invitation to unite our sufferings to his as we sing or read "Let me mingle tears with thee, / Mourning him who mourned for me."[1] We journey alongside women of history with Mary the Mother of Christ, Mary Magdalene, Veronica, and the weeping women of Jerusalem. We encounter, we encourage, we console, we grieve.

What better prayer can we pray than to move through the space and time of pregnancy, awaiting its climax, than the Way of the Cross, the path through which life comes to those who believe?

THE FIRST STATION
Jesus Is Condemned to Death

To begin, enter into the Presence of God, and beseech him to inspire you.

In the name of the Father, the Son, and the Holy Spirit. We adore you, O Christ, and we praise you, (*genuflect or bow*) because by your holy cross you have redeemed the world.

Jesus my Lord, my God, my all!

Read

> Pilate entered the praetorium again and called Jesus, and said to him, "Are you the King of the Jews?" Jesus answered, "Do you say this of your own accord, or did others say it to you about me?" Pilate answered, "Am I a Jew? Your own nation and the chief priests have handed you over to me; what have you done?" Jesus answered, "My kingship is not of this world; if my kingship were of this world, my servants would fight, that I might not be handed over to the Jews; but my kingship is not from the world." Pilate said to him, "So you are a king?" Jesus answered, "You say that I am a king. For this I was born, and for this I have come into the world, to bear witness to the truth. Every one who is of the truth hears my voice." Pilate said to him, "What is truth?"

When the chief priests and the officers saw him, they cried out, "Crucify him, crucify him!" Pilate said to them, "Take him yourselves and crucify him, for I find no crime in him." The Jews answered him, "We have a law, and by that law he ought to die, because he has made himself the Son of God." When Pilate heard these words, he was even more afraid; he entered the praetorium again and said to Jesus, "Where are you from?" But Jesus gave no answer. Pilate therefore said to him, "You will not speak to me? Do you not know that I have power to release you, and power to crucify you?" Jesus answered him, "You would have no power over me unless it had been given you from above; therefore he who delivered me to you has the greater sin."

Upon this Pilate sought to release him, but the Jews cried out, "If you release this man, you are not Caesar's friend; every one who makes himself a king sets himself against Caesar." When Pilate heard these words, he brought Jesus out and sat down on the judgment seat at a place called The Pavement, and in Hebrew, Gabbatha. Now it was the day of Preparation of the Passover; it was about the sixth hour. He said to the Jews, "Here is your King!" They cried out, "Away with him, away with him, crucify him!" Pilate said to them, "Shall I crucify your King?" The chief priests answered, "We have no king but Caesar." Then he handed him over to them to be crucified. (John 18:33–38; 19:6–16)

Pray

Lord, your kingdom is not of this world, and this world does not have the power to free us. It is in your kingdom alone that I discover freedom — the freedom to choose how to respond to the circumstances that lay before me. This is truth. Your word is truth. *Ecce homo*! Behold the man! In silence, in speech, you stood in peace, condemned to suffer that we might be saved.

Lord Jesus Christ, Son of the living God, have mercy on me, a sinner. Amen.

At the cross her station keeping,
Stood the mournful Mother weeping,
close to Jesus to the last.

Through her heart, his sorrow sharing,
All his bitter anguish bearing,
Now at length the sword has passed.

THE SECOND STATION
Jesus Carries His Cross

We adore you, O Christ, and we praise you, (*genuflect or bow*)
because by your holy cross you have redeemed the world.

Jesus my Lord, my God, my all!

Read

From that time Jesus began to show his disciples that
he must go to Jerusalem and suffer many things from
the elders and chief priests and scribes, and be killed,
and on the third day be raised. And Peter took him and
began to rebuke him, saying, "God forbid, Lord! This
shall never happen to you." But he turned and said to
Peter, "Get behind me, Satan! You are a hindrance to
me; for you are not on the side of God, but of men."
(Matthew 16:21–23)

So they took Jesus, and he went out, bearing his own
cross, to the place called the place of a skull, which is
called in Hebrew Golgotha. (John 19:17)

Pray

Who can know the mind of God (see Rom 11:34)? Lord, you
turned our human interpretation of suffering and power on its

head. The world perceives adversity as a punishment. Yet you chose to take on humanity's flesh, representing us in a covenant with God, and to offer yourself as an impeccable sacrifice to the Father. Then you commanded us to be perfect as your Father is perfect, in love for God and neighbor, in self-offering as we take up our cross and follow you. It is only through a sincere gift of self that I can truly find myself.[2]

Lord Jesus Christ, Son of the living God, have mercy on me, a sinner. Amen.

Oh, how sad and sore distressed
Was that Mother highly blessed,
Of the sole begotten One!

Christ above in torment hangs;
She beneath beholds the pangs
Of her dying, glorious Son.

THE THIRD STATION
Jesus Falls the First Time

We adore you, O Christ, and we praise you, (*genuflect or bow*)
because by your holy cross you have redeemed the world.
Jesus my Lord, my God, my all!

Read

Surely he has borne our griefs
and carried our sorrows;
yet we esteemed him stricken,
struck down by God, and afflicted.
But he was wounded for our transgressions,
he was bruised for our iniquities;
upon him was the chastisement that made us whole,
and with his stripes we are healed.
All we like sheep have gone astray;
we have turned every one to his own way;
and the LORD has laid on him
the iniquity of us all.

He was oppressed, and he was afflicted,
yet he opened not his mouth;
like a lamb that is led to the slaughter,
and like a sheep that before its shearers is silent,

so he opened not his mouth. (Isaiah 53:4–7)

Pray

You fell, my Lord, but you did not falter. Your will remained the same, regardless of your physical weakness. You bore the scourging, the whips, the spittle from the people who had so recently praised your Name. You might have said this was the end, but you would not stop. You would fall; you would rise. In total commitment to the Father's will, you had no other choice but to continue. Lord, help me also to keep a peaceful heart even in the hardest moments.

Lord Jesus Christ, Son of the living God, have mercy on me, a sinner. Amen.

Is there one who would not weep,
'Whelmed in miseries so deep,
Christ's dear Mother to behold?

Can the human heart refrain
From partaking in her pain,
In that Mother's pain untold?

THE FOURTH STATION
Jesus Meets Mary, His Mother

We adore you, O Christ, and we praise you, (*genuflect or bow*)
because by your holy cross you have redeemed the world.

Jesus my Lord, my God, my all!

Read

Simeon blessed them and said to Mary his mother …

"(and a sword will pierce through your own soul also),
that thoughts out of many hearts may be revealed." …

A woman in the crowd raised her voice and said to [Jesus], "Blessed is the womb that bore you, and the breasts that you sucked!" But he said, "Blessed rather are those who hear the word of God and keep it!" (Luke 2:34–35; 11:27)

"Is it nothing to you, all you who pass by?
Look and see
if there is any sorrow like my sorrow." (Lamentations 1:12)

Pray

Lord Jesus Christ, as you reached your mother on the way, she held all these things in her heart (see Lk 2:19). There was no suffering you could hide from her. She carried you. She would have carried you now on this last journey. She grieved more because she could not relieve your pain. Mary was the first who received your Flesh and Blood into her body. She was the first to cradle your body, vulnerable and breakable, in her hands. She was the one whose sacrifices reflected the apostle's path from liberation from original sin to a resurrected body in heaven. You faced each other at this point on your journey to Golgotha, but one day she came to sit beside you at the throne of God. The scars of her body and her heart were not erased but rather were brought to glory in transcendent suffering. Yet at this moment — as she suffers alongside your ordeal — all of this goes unseen. All these promises hide in hope within her Immaculate Heart. Lord, teach me to love as she loved, to give as she gave.

Lord Jesus Christ, Son of the living God, have mercy on me, a sinner. Amen.

Bruised, derided, cursed, defiled,
She beheld her tender Child,
All with bloody scourges rent.

THE FIFTH STATION
Simon of Cyrene Helps Jesus Carry His Cross

We adore you, O Christ, and we praise you, (*genuflect or bow*)
because by your holy cross you have redeemed the world.

Jesus my Lord, my God, my all!

Read

> And as they led him away, they seized one Simon of
> Cyrene, who was coming in from the country, and laid
> on him the cross, to carry it behind Jesus. (Luke 23:26)

> Then Jesus told his disciples, "If any man would come
> after me, let him deny himself and take up his cross and
> follow me. For whoever would save his life will lose it,
> and whoever loses his life for my sake will find it. For
> what will it profit a man, if he gains the whole world and
> forfeits his life? Or what shall a man give in return for
> his life? For the Son of man is to come with his angels
> in the glory of his Father, and then he will repay every
> man for what he has done. Truly, I say to you, there are
> some standing here who will not taste death before they
> see the Son of man coming in his kingdom." (Matthew
> 16:24–28)

Prayer

Lord, Simon was violently compelled to join in your passion. You are perfect, and yet you did not bear this alone. Son of Man, Son of God, you bore your body to be weakened to the point that you could not carry your cross. Another was forced to lift it for you. Your sacrificial gift is not diminished by accepting another's help. When I falter, support me, Lord. Reveal to me those you have sent to help me along this way.

Lord Jesus Christ, Son of the living God, have mercy on me, a sinner. Amen.

For the sins of his own nation,
Saw him hang in desolation
till His Spirit forth he sent.

THE SIXTH STATION
Veronica Wipes the Face of Jesus

We adore you, O Christ, and we praise you, (*genuflect or bow*)
because by your holy cross you have redeemed the world.

Jesus my Lord, my God, my all!

Read

Moses said, "I beg you, show me your glory." And he
said, "I will make all my goodness pass before you, and
will proclaim before you my name 'The LORD'; and I
will be gracious to whom I will be gracious, and will
show mercy on whom I will show mercy. But," he said,
"you cannot see my face; for man shall not see me and
live." And the LORD said, "Behold, there is a place by
me where you shall stand upon the rock; and while my
glory passes by I will put you in a cleft of the rock, and I
will cover you with my hand until I have passed by; then
I will take away my hand, and you shall see my back; but
my face shall not be seen." (Exodus 33:18–23)

Prayer

God of Israel, if I pray, "Show me your glory," what will I see?
A power wrapped so tightly in humility it suffered itself to be
wrapped in swaddling clothes by a Virgin in a cave? In response

to an act of mercy performed by a woman whose true name we do not know, you left the image of your divine glory — the glory of complete and total abandonment to the will of God your Father — wrapped in fragments of cloth. On Veronica's veil, you bequeathed an image of your holy face.

Lord Jesus Christ, Son of the living God, have mercy on me, a sinner. Amen.

O, sweet Mother! fount of love,
Touch my spirit from above,
Make my heart with yours accord.

THE SEVENTH STATION
Jesus Falls for the Second Time

We adore you, O Christ, and we praise you, (*genuflect or bow*)
because by your holy cross you have redeemed the world.

Jesus my Lord, my God, my all!

Read

I am utterly bowed down and prostrate;
all the day I go about mourning.
For my loins are filled with burning,
and there is no soundness in my flesh.
I am utterly spent and crushed;
I groan because of the tumult of my heart.
Lord, all my longing is known to you,
my sighing is not hidden from you.
My heart throbs, my strength fails me;
and the light of my eyes — it also has gone from me.
My friends and companions stand aloof from my plague,
and my kinsmen stand afar off.
But for you, O LORD, do I wait;
it is you, O LORD my God,
who will answer. (Psalm 38:6–11, 15)

Pray

Even with Simon's aid, you fell to the ground again. The strain bore your worn body down. Fatigue, sleeplessness, blood loss, and heartache weighed down your figure until your knees crashed to the stone pavement. Your arms lay at your side, covered in dust and blood as you gathered, with a firm will, your strength to straighten them, kneel, stand, and continue. God's power is made perfect in weakness (see 2 Cor 12:9). Fr. Jacques Philippe wisely tells us, "The real spiritual battle, rather than the pursuit of the invincibility or some other absolute infallibility beyond our capacity, consists principally in learning, without becoming too discouraged, to accept falling occasionally and not to lose our peace of heart if we should happen to do so lamentably."[3] Let me hold this idea in my heart, as I see that even you, my God, fell along the way.

Lord Jesus Christ, Son of the living God, have mercy on me, a sinner. Amen.

Make me feel as you have felt;
Make my soul to glow and melt
With the love of Christ, my Lord.

THE EIGHTH STATION
Jesus Meets the Women of Jerusalem

We adore you, O Christ, and we praise you, (*genuflect or bow*)
because by your holy cross you have redeemed the world.

Jesus my Lord, my God, my all!

Read

And there followed him a great multitude of the people,
and of women who bewailed and lamented him. But Jesus turning to them said, "Daughters of Jerusalem, do
not weep for me, but weep for yourselves and for your
children." (Luke 23:27–28)

But Ruth said, "Entreat me not to leave you or to return from following you; for where you go I will go, and
where you lodge I will lodge; your people shall be my
people, and your God my God." (Ruth 1:16)

Behold, I will bring them from the north country,
and gather them from the farthest parts of the
    earth,
among them the blind and the lame,
the woman with child and her who has labor
    pains, together;

a great company, they shall return here.
With weeping they shall come,
and with consolations I will lead them back.
I will turn their mourning into joy,
I will comfort them, and give them gladness for
sorrow. (Jeremiah 31:8–9, 13)

Pray

Jesus, the women attended to you on the way to Golgotha. They were the women who shadowed you on the road in ministry and miracles, women who provided for your needs (see Lk 8:3). Now they followed you in anguish, pushing on until it was finished. Your pledge remained with them; their faith remained with you. Like these women and you, I walk with my child; I would pour myself out for this child. Meet me in this love. Show me how to travel this way of love.

Lord Jesus Christ, Son of the living God, have mercy on me, a sinner. Amen.

Holy Mother, pierce me through,
In my heart each wound renew
Of my Savior crucified.

THE NINTH STATION
Jesus Falls for the Third Time

We adore you, O Christ, and we praise you, (*genuflect or bow*)
because by your holy cross you have redeemed the world.
Jesus my Lord, my God, my all!

Read

In all their affliction he was afflicted,
and the angel of his presence saved them;
in his love and in his pity he redeemed them;
he lifted them up and carried them all the days of
old. (Isaiah 63:9)

For he will give his angels charge of you
to guard you in all your ways.
On their hands they will bear you up,
lest you dash your foot against a stone.
You will tread on the lion and the adder,
the young lion and the serpent you will trample
under foot.
Because he clings to me in love, I will deliver him;
I will protect him, because he knows my name.

When he calls to me, I will answer him;

I will be with him in trouble,
I will rescue him and honor him.
With long life I will satisfy him,
and show him my salvation. (Psalm 91:11–16)

Pray

My God, was there no mercy? When would this agonizing day end? To plunge again and yet be so close, extended beyond your capacity. Completion would do nothing to relieve your injury now. Dropping, filled with weariness — rising sounds worse. What lay ahead on your road to Calvary? How could you bear it any longer?

You persevered. That you could fall and rise a first, then a second, and then a third time without despair maps the path for our lives. Father Philippe says, "We will be saints the day when our inabilities and our nothingness will no longer be for us a subject of sadness and anxiety, but a subject of peace and joy."[4]

I need not be surprised that I struggle. Give me your grace in my response to the struggle.

Lord Jesus Christ, Son of the living God, have mercy on me, a sinner. Amen.

Let me share with you his pain,
Who for all our sins was slain,
Who for me in torments died.

THE TENTH STATION:
Jesus Is Stripped of His Clothes

We adore you, O Christ, and we praise you, (*genuflect or bow*) because by your holy cross you have redeemed the world.

Jesus my Lord, my God, my all!

Read

I can count all my bones —
they stare and gloat over me;
they divide my garments among them,
and for my clothing they cast lots. (Psalm 22:17–18)

And Jesus said, "Father, forgive them; for they know not what they do." And they cast lots to divide his garments. (Luke 23:34)

Prayer

The course toward Calvary was over. You arrived there, stripped naked, clothes commandeered by strangers. Your body lay open for all to see in its agony. Oh, my Lord and my God!

Lord Jesus Christ, Son of the living God, have mercy on me, a sinner. Amen.

Let me mingle tears with thee,
Mourning Him Who mourned for me,
All the days that I may live.

THE ELEVENTH STATION
Jesus Is Nailed to the Cross

We adore you, O Christ, and we praise you, (*genuflect or bow*) because by your holy cross you have redeemed the world.

Jesus my Lord, my God, my all!

Read

They have pierced my hands and feet. (Psalm 22:16)

There they crucified him, and with him two others, one on either side, and Jesus between them. (John 19:18)

There was also an inscription over him, "This is the King of the Jews."

One of the criminals who were hanged railed at him, saying, "Are you not the Christ? Save yourself and us!" But the other rebuked him, saying, "Do you not fear God, since you are under the same sentence of condemnation? And we indeed justly; for we are receiving the due reward of our deeds; but this man has done nothing wrong." And he said, "Jesus, remember me when you come in your kingly power." And he said to him, "Truly, I say to you, today you will be with me in Paradise." (Luke 23:38–43)

But standing by the cross of Jesus were his mother, and his mother's sister, Mary the wife of Clopas, and Mary Magdalene. When Jesus saw his mother, and the disciple whom he loved standing near, he said to his mother, "Woman, behold, your son!" Then he said to the disciple, "Behold, your mother!" And from that hour the disciple took her to his own home. (John 19:25–27)

Prayer
Nails punctured your wrists and feet. All who loved you stood transfixed. You extended your Sacred Heart, gasping for breath, to protect and console those whom you loved: the repentant thief, the beloved disciple, the Mother of Sorrows who kept your secrets in her heart. As your passion reached its apex, your heart swelled with a love directed toward humanity. In your agony, you existed wholly for me, for all humanity.

Lord Jesus Christ, Son of the living God, have mercy on me, a sinner. Amen.

By the cross with you to stay,
There with you to weep and pray,
This I ask of you to give.

TWELFTH STATION
Jesus Dies on the Cross

We adore you, O Christ, and we praise you, (*genuflect or bow*)
because by your holy cross you have redeemed the world.
>Jesus my Lord, my God, my all!

Read
>Now from the sixth hour there was darkness over all
>the land until the ninth hour. And about the ninth
>hour Jesus cried with a loud voice, "Eli, Eli, la'ma sa-
>bach'-tha'ni?" that is, "My God, my God, why have you
>forsaken me?" And some of the bystanders hearing it
>said, "This man is calling Elijah." And one of them at
>once ran and took a sponge, filled it with vinegar, and
>put it on a reed, and gave it to him to drink. But the
>others said, "Wait, let us see whether Elijah will come to
>save him." And Jesus cried again with a loud voice and
>yielded up his spirit. (Matthew 27:45–50)

>My God, my God, why have you forsaken me?
>>Why are you so far from helping me, from the
>>>words of my groaning?
>O my God, I cry by day, but you do not answer;
>>and by night, but find no rest.

Yet you are holy,
>enthroned on the praises of Israel.

In you our fathers trusted;
>they trusted, and you delivered them.

To you they cried, and were saved;
>in you they trusted, and were not disappointed.

But you, O LORD, be not far off!
>O my help, hasten to my aid! (Psalm 22:1–5, 19)

Prayer

Richard John Neuhaus tells us about hope: "Hope is faith disposed toward the future; it is faith holding on; it is faith holding out; it is faith defiantly, trustingly, hurled into the present absence; it is handing over our hopelessness. 'Father, into your hands I commend my spirit.'"[5]

Lord, with a cry you gave yourself into your Father's hands. You descended into the dead; you released righteous captives awaiting redemption with a blessed hope. In the silence after your exclamation, could anyone understand? Could anyone perceive the world shaking at the death of God, at the gates of heaven opening, at the beginning of the kingdom of God?

When my time comes to deliver this child, be beside me, Christ, and let me offer you all I have to give.

Lord Jesus Christ, Son of the living God, have mercy on me, a sinner. Amen.

Virgin, of all virgins blest,
O refuse not my request:
let me in thy weeping share.

Let me, to my latest breath,
in my body bear the death
of that dying Son of thine.[6]

THE THIRTEENTH STATION
Jesus Is Taken Down from the Cross

We adore you, O Christ, and we praise you, (*genuflect or bow*) because by your holy cross you have redeemed the world.

Jesus my Lord, my God, my all!

Read

But one of the soldiers pierced his side with a spear, and at once there came out blood and water. (Jn 19:34)

Now there was a man named Joseph from the Jewish town of Arimathea. He was a member of the council, a good and righteous man, who had not consented to their purpose and deed, and he was looking for the kingdom of God. This man went to Pilate and asked for the body of Jesus. Then he took it down and wrapped it in a linen shroud. (Luke 23:50–53)

Pray

Lord, your heart was pierced with a lance from which poured mercy and redemption.

Your mother's heart was pierced with seven sorrows.[7]

Your lifeless body dropped into her arms. Mary held you. She cleaved to you, but you were beyond her now.

Mary drew close to her child's body as a mother's body was ever meant to do. Her arms wrapped around you as her hands grasped the face of the Son she loved so well.

Just so, my own child's life is written into the very fabric of my being. May I treasure this mystery through all life's stages.

Lord Jesus Christ, Son of the living God, have mercy on me, a sinner. Amen.

Wounded with his every wound,
steep my soul till it hath swooned
in His very blood away.

Be to me, o Virgin, nigh,
lest in flames I burn and die,
in that awful judgment day.

THE FOURTEENTH STATION
Jesus Is Placed in the Tomb

We adore you, O Christ, and we praise you, (*genuflect or bow*) because by your holy cross you have redeemed the world.

Jesus my Lord, my God, my all!

Read

And Joseph took the body, and wrapped it in a clean linen shroud, and laid it in his own new tomb, which he had hewn in the rock; and he rolled a great stone to the door of the tomb, and departed. Mary Magdalene and the other Mary were there, sitting opposite the tomb. (Matthew 27:59–61)

The women who had come with him from Galilee followed, and saw the tomb, and how his body was laid; then they returned, and prepared spices and ointments. (Luke 23:55)

Pray

Your agony passed. Your body rested in the tomb, guarded by angels. With tender devotion, the women who loved you prepared to treat your body for burial. They lovingly cleaned and ministered the battered body of you, their Lord. They completed every merciful duty in burying the dead. They honored you as king. They waited.

Mary bore you in a borrowed stable. These women prepared for you a borrowed tomb. Yet when they arrived, after all that had passed, they did not encounter the living among the dead.

May my motherhood reflect such tender love and endless hope.

Lord Jesus Christ, Son of the living God, have mercy on me, a sinner. Amen.

Christ, when thou shalt call me hence,
be Thy mother my defense,
be Thy cross my victory.

While my body here decays,
may my soul Thy goodness praise,
safe in Paradise with Thee. Amen.

VI

Night Prayer

The Liturgy of the Hours is a prayer of the Church, described directly in the *Catechism of the Catholic Church* (see 1174–1178). It is one way in which we can "pray constantly," as Saint Paul called us to do (1 Thes 5:17), by praying throughout the day at particular hours. According to the *Catechism*, through the Liturgy of the Hours, "The mystery of Christ, his Incarnation and Passover, which we celebrate in the Eucharist especially at the Sunday assembly, permeates and transfigures the time of each day" (1174).

Sleep can be elusive during pregnancy, particularly in our last trimester. Compline, or Night Prayer, as the last prayer of the day, can help us to especially unite with the Lord during this sleepless time.

The references to night during Compline symbolize more than just physical sleep. Night can represent adversity, isolation, or suffering. When the external demands of the day have ceased, we are alone with our thoughts and our emotions. Sleep is not only restorative; it is a quiet vulnerability. As silence grows during the night, our body communicates more loudly. Our heart attends to the movements of our baby. Everything feels heightened at night.

This time awakens our senses. The references to death in Compline are intended to alert us to life's dangers and to the need to draw near the Lord and direct our lives to him. When we pray the psalms, we entrust our heart to God and remind ourselves of God's vast power, mercy, and love.

In Night Prayer, we repeat the words of the psalmist and Christ on the cross: "Into your hands, Lord, I commend my spirit" (see Lk 23:46). The antiphon "Protect us Lord" is a poetic supplication to God for protection at all moments of the day and night. On its own, it is a beautiful prayer to say before bed or when rising; consider memorizing it or writing it on a slip of paper to keep at your bedside table. The Canticle of Simeon praises God for a hope fulfilled and waiting rewarded, even after longing for many years. We can turn our gaze to Mary as she hears his words and takes them into her heart. How apt this vision becomes for us as expectant mothers! The prayer concludes with an antiphon to Our Lady, through whose life we see the blessing and reward of motherhood so clearly.

In its structure, repetition, and universality the Liturgy of the Hours leads us into something larger than ourselves, something secure and enveloping, beyond the prayers we pray privately. In it, we pray with the words of Sacred Scripture, we sit at the saints' feet, and we pray at the foot of the cross.

In your search for peace during pregnancy, I invite you to integrate Night Prayer into the rhythm of your day. In the following pages you will find Sunday's Night Prayer. While following the same format, each weekday offers a different focus and difference Scriptures, which can be found in print or online (see Universalis. com or iBreviary.com, as well as many others).

God, come to my assistance.
— Lord, make haste to help me.

Glory to the Father, and to the Son,
and to the Holy Spirit:
— as it was in the beginning, is now,
and will be for ever. Amen.

Take a moment to make a brief examination of conscience.

Sing or recite your favorite hymn — the Liturgy of the Hours suggests "Now that the Daylight Dies Away."

Antiphon: Night holds no terrors for me sleeping under God's wings.

(Psalm 91)
He who dwells in the shelter of the Most High

and abides in the shade of the Almighty
says to the Lord: "My refuge,
my stronghold, my God in whom I trust!"
It is he who will free you from the snare
of the fowler who seeks to destroy you;
he will conceal you with his pinions
and under his wings you will find refuge.
You will not fear the terror of the night
nor the arrow that flies by day,
nor the plague that prowls in the darkness
nor the scourge that lays waste at noon.
A thousand may fall at your side,
ten thousand fall at your right,
you, it will never approach;
his faithfulness is buckler and shield.
Your eyes have only to look
to see how the wicked are repaid,
you who have said: "Lord, my refuge!"
and have made the Most High your dwelling.
Upon you no evil shall fall,
no plague approach where you dwell.
For you has he commanded his angels,
to keep you in all your ways.
They shall bear you upon their hands
lest you strike your foot against a stone.

On the lion and the viper you will tread
and trample the young lion and the dragon.
Since he clings to me in love, I will free him;
protect him for he knows my name.
When he calls I shall answer: "I am with you."
I will save him in distress and give him glory.
With length of life I will content him;
I shall let him see my saving power.
Glory be to the Father, and to the Son,
and to the Holy Spirit:
as it was in the beginning, is now,
and will be for ever. Amen.

Repeat antiphon: Night holds no terrors for me sleeping under God's wings.

Reading
Revelation 22:4–5
They shall see the Lord face to face and bear his name on their foreheads. The night shall be no more. They will need no light from lamps or the sun, for the Lord God shall give them light, and they shall reign forever.

Responsory
Into your hands, O Lord, I commend my spirit.

— Into your hands, O Lord, I commend my spirit.
You have redeemed us, Lord God of truth.
— I commend my spirit.
Glory to the Father, and to the Son, and to the Holy Spirit,
— Into your hands, O Lord, I commend my spirit.

Gospel Canticle

Antiphon: Protect us Lord, as we stay awake; watch over us as we sleep, that awake, we may keep watch with Christ, and asleep, rest in his peace.

Luke 2:29–32
Lord, now you let your servant go in peace;
your word has been fulfilled:
my own eyes have seen the salvation
which you have prepared in the sight of every people:
a light to reveal you to the nations
and the glory of your people Israel.

Glory be to the Father, and to the Son,
and to the Holy Spirit:
as it was in the beginning, is now,
and will be for ever. Amen.

Repeat antiphon: Protect us Lord, as we stay awake; watch over us as we sleep, that awake, we may keep watch with Christ, and asleep, rest in his peace.

Prayer

Lord, we beg you to visit this house and banish from it all the deadly power of the enemy.

May your holy angels dwell here to keep us in peace, and may your blessing be upon us always.

We ask this through Christ Our Lord. Amen.

May the all-powerful Lord grant us a restful night and a peaceful death. Amen.

Antiphon to Our Lady

Hail, holy Queen, Mother of mercy,
our life, our sweetness and our hope.
To you do we cry, poor banished children of Eve.
To you do we send up our sighs
mourning and weeping in this vale of tears.
Turn then, most gracious advocate, your eyes of mercy toward us,
and after this our exile
show unto us the blessed fruit of thy womb, Jesus.
O clement, O loving,
O sweet Virgin Mary.

INDEX OF SACRED ART

NOTES

I. Reflections on Peace

1. Hilary S. Gammill and J. Lee Nelson, "Naturally Acquired Microchimerism." *The International Journal of Developmental Biology*, 54 (2010): 531–543, https://doi.org/10.1387/ijdb.082767hg.

2. *Catechism of the Catholic Church*, 2nd ed. (Vatican, Libreria Editrice Vaticana, 2012), 41. Hereafter cited in text.

II. Portraits of Peace in Holy Mothers

1. Paul Burns, ed., *Butler's Lives of the Saints: New Concise Edition*, (Collegeville, MN: Liturgical Press, 2003), 384.

2. Fr. Alban Butler, *The Lives of the Fathers, Martyrs, and Other Principal* Saints, vol. 3 (London: Virtue & Co., 1936), 940.

3. Burns, ed., *Butler's Lives of the Saints*, 385.

4. "Mother Teresa: Acceptance Speech," The Nobel Prize, Nobel Prize Outreach AB, https://www.nobelprize.org/prizes/peace/1979/teresa/26200-mother-teresa-acceptance-speech-1979/.

5. Giovanni Falbo, *Saint Monica: The Power of a Mother's Love*, (Boston: Pauline Books & Media, 2007), 22.

6. Ibid., 41.

7. Ibid., 46.

8. Marie-Michel Philipon, OP, *Conchita: A Mother's Spiritual Diary*

(New York: Alba House, 1978), 39.

9. Ibid., 37.

10. Ibid., 30

11. St. Gianna Beretta Molla, *Love Letters to My Husband*, ed. Elio Guerriero (Boston: Pauline Books & Media, 2002), 80.

12. Ibid., 62.

13. Ibid., 124.

14. Sts. Louis & Zélie Martin, *A Call to a Deeper Love: The Family Correspondence of the Parents of Saint Thérèse of the Child Jesus (1864–1885)*, (New York: Society of St. Paul, 2011), 26.

15. St. Thérèse of the Child Jesus, *Story of a Soul: The Autobiography of St. Thérèse of Lisieux*, (Rockford, IL: TAN Books, 1997), 13.

16. Ibid.

17. Simone Troisi and Cristiana Paccini, *Chiara Corbella Petrillo: A Witness of Joy*, (Manchester, New Hampshire, Sophia Institute Press, 2015), 29.

18. Ibid., 8.

19. Ibid., 122.

20. Ibid.,127.

21. Ibid.

III. Prayers of Peace

1. Charles J. Callan, OP and John A. McHugh, OP, *Blessed be God: A Complete Catholic Prayer Book*, (New York, P. J. Kenedy & Sons, 1959), cited in "Morning Prayers," The Catholic Database Project, catholicdatabase.com, https://catholicdatabase.com/prayers/morningprayers.php.

2. Ibid.

3. "Prayer of Cardinal Newman," John Henry Newman — Prayers, John Henry Newman Catholic College, https:/www.johnhenrynewmancatholiccollege.org.uk/john-henry-newman-prayers/.

4. "Sequence — Veni, Sancte Spiritus," Pentecost Sunday — Mass During the Day, May 24, 2015, Daily Readings, United States Conference of Catholic Bishops, https://bible.usccb.org/bible/readings/052415-pentecost-day.cfm.

5. "Catholic Prayer: Canticle of the Sun," Catholic Culture, Trinity Communications, https://www.catholicculture.org/culture/liturgicalyear/prayers/view.cfm?id=872.

6. St. Teresa of Ávila, "Prayer of Saint Teresa of Avila," Eternal Word Television Network, https://www.ewtn.com/catholicism/devotions/prayer-of-saint-teresa-of-avila-364.

IV. Reflections on the Rosary

1. John Paul II, *Rosarium Virginis Mariae*, 2021, Vatican.va, par. 10.

2. Ibid., par. 21.

3. Ibid., par. 22.

4. Ibid.

5. Paul VI, *Gaudium et Spes*, Vatican.va, par. 24.

6. "The first goal of spiritual combat, that toward which our efforts must above all else be directed, is not to always obtain a victory (over our temptations, our weaknesses, etc.), rather it is to learn to maintain peace of heart under all circumstances, even in the case of defeat." Fr. Jacques Philippe, *Searching for and Maintaining Peace: A Small Treatise on Peace of Heart*, trans. George and Jannic Driscoll (New York: Alba House, 2002), 12.

7. St. John of Damascene, *Dormition of Mary*, homily 2, no. 14, in Patrologiae Cursus Completus: Series Graeca, ed. J.-P. Migne (Paris), 96, 741. Translation taken from the second reading of the Office of Readings for the Assumption, August 15, in the Liturgy of the Hours.

V. Stations of the Cross

1. Text for this and following stanzas taken from "At The Cross Her Station Keeping," Hymnary.org, https://hymnary.org/text/at_the_cross_her_station_keeping_stood.

2. See Paul VI, *GS*, par. 24.

3. Philippe, *Searching for and Maintaining Peace*, 12.

4. Ibid., 80.

5. Richard John Neuhaus, *Death on a Friday Afternoon: Meditations on the Last Words of Jesus from the Cross* (New York: Basic Books, 2001), 233.

6. This and stanzas for the final stations are taken from "Stabat Mater — English Translation," The Ultimate Stabat Mater Website, https://stabatmater.info/stabat-mater-english-translation/.

7. See Marge Fenelon, "What Are the Seven Sorrows of Mary?," National Catholic Register, Eternal Word Television Network, September 15, 2017, http://www.ncregister.com/blog/mfenelon/what -are-the-seven-sorrows-of-mary.

About the Author

Kathryn Anne Casey is a published author, journalist, farmer-florist, home educator, former life coach and prevention specialist, wife of twelve years, and mother of five children here on earth and four in heaven (three by miscarriage and one stillborn caused by anencephaly). Her youngest son has a rare genetic mutation called SPINT2 and is TPN dependent.

Kathryn served a year with the National Evangelization Team, holds a B.A. in Psychology from the University of St. Thomas in Minnesota, and a M.S. in Clinical Psychology from the Institute for the Psychological Sciences, now Divine Mercy University. She is the author of *Journey in Love: A Catholic Mother's Prayers after Prenatal Diagnosis* and *Peace in Pregnancy: Devotions for the Expectant Mother*. She is a journalist and regular columnist for the Hughson Chronicle & Denair Dispatch.

Kathryn grew up in Hughson, California, and lived briefly in Minnesota and Virginia before returning home with her husband and firstborn to be near family. When her son, Peter, was hospitalized in 2016, life began to look radically different and every step since then has been an act finding God's will in the small events of the day-to-day. Kathryn now lives just outside of Hughson on an acre of land with her husband, children, cats, chickens, turkeys, and flowers.